Historic Walks
in and around
Birmingham

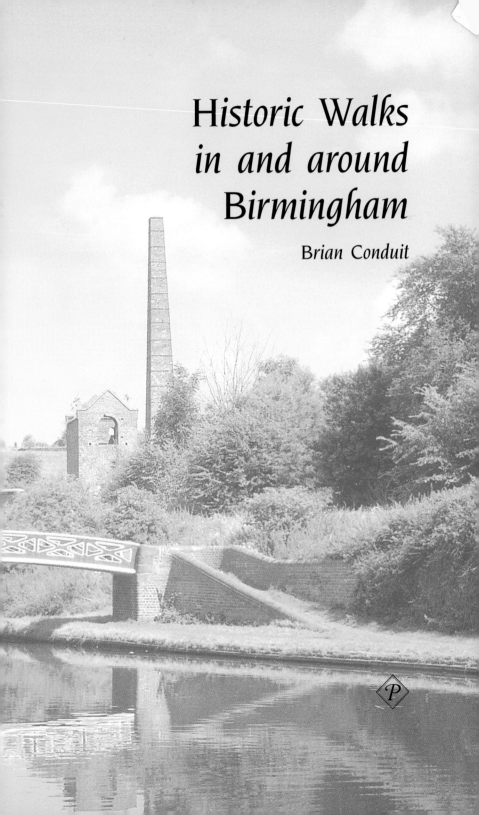

Historic Walks
in and around
Birmingham

Brian Conduit

First published in 2008
by Palatine Books,
Carnegie House,
Chatsworth Road
Lancaster LA1 4SL
www.palatinebooks.com

British Library Cataloguing-in-Publication data
A catalogue record for this book is available from the British Library

ISBN: 978-1-874181-51-4

Designed and typeset by Carnegie Book Production
www.carnegiebookproduction.com

Printed and bound in the UK by Alden Press

Contents

M6

Stafford

M42

⑫

⑪

M54

⑳

⑯

⑩

⑨

⑳

Wolverhampton

BIRMINGHAM

Nuneaton

⑤

⑲

⑧

④

①

② ③

⑥

Coventry

⑱

⑦

⑰

㉒

⑬

⑮

Worcester

⑭

Stratford-upon-Avon

㉓

㉑

Evesham

M40

㉔

M5

Introduction to Birmingham and the surrounding area

In the 1860s, Elihu Burritt, then the US Consul in Birmingham, wrote a book called 'Walks in the Black Country and Its Green Borderland'. This was an account of his travels through the area around Birmingham, carried out not only as part of his consular duties but also because he was fascinated by the area, both by its industries and by the 'green borderland' that encircled the industrial zone. Both the Black Country and its green borderland are the subjects of this walking guide which takes you through one of the most interesting as well as one of the most attractive parts of Britain.

Birmingham is principally a product of the Industrial Revolution. Before that it was a relatively small and insignificant place, less important than nearby towns such as Warwick which it has since greatly outstripped. By the sixteenth century small scale metal working industries had become established there, as a result of the proximity of the coal and iron deposits of the Black Country, and by the time of the Civil War in the 1640s it had acquired a reputation as a manufacturer of small arms.

It has always been Birmingham's claim that it has more miles of canal than Venice, and this may well be true. The canals played a major role in the tremendous growth of the city in the eighteenth and nineteenth centuries when it became one of the world's great manufacturing centres, widely known as 'the city of a thousand trades' These artificial waterways were essential because Birmingham lacks a navigable river and the city became the hub of the nation's canal network. Since the decline of commercial traffic on the canals, they have been restored, cleaned up and become one of Birmingham's principal recreational assets, the focal points of several rejuvenated areas around the city centre.

During the late nineteenth century a number of splendid civic monuments were erected and the municipal enterprise of the Chamberlain era caused one American visitor to describe Birmingham as the best governed city in the world. By 1931 it had become the second city in the country, a title it has maintained since. Birmingham's motto is 'Forward' and the city has always been in the forefront of change and development. This has not always worked to its advantage as some years ago it was plagued by some of the worst of 1960s architecture and condemned as a place that had sacrificed itself to the motor car and in the process had swept away much of its fine Victorian architecture. This has now changed and in recent years Birmingham has been transformed through a series of impressive modern developments, while at the same time conserving and enhancing its remaining Victorian buildings.

The Black Country lies to the west. It acquired its name from the pall of smoke that used to hang over the area at the height of the Industrial Revolution but the coal mines have closed, much of its heavy industry has gone and the area has become much cleaner and greener. As in Brmingham, the many canals that criss-cross the area are not only used for pleasure boating but also make excellent walking and cycling routes.

Surrounding the industrial zone is Burritt's green borderland. Close at hand are the wooded slopes of the Lickey and Clent Hills and the open expanses of Sutton Park. A little further away remnants of the ancient forests that once covered much of the area, supplemented by newer plantations, survive in Cannock Chase, Wyre Forest and the woodlands of Arden. Mention of the Forest of Arden inevitably leads on to Stratford and the Avon valley, the area known as Shakespeare Country. It is not only the fame of Shakespeare but the unspoilt landscape, old towns and villages and thatched black and white Tudor buildings that attract visitors to this delightful region. From Shakespeare Country the Avon flows through the blossom and fruit growing country of the Vale of Evesham to join the River Severn, whose banks are graced by a series of attractive old towns that include Bewdley, Stourport and the cathedral city of Worcester.

The major historic attractions of the area include the superb medieval cathedrals of Lichfield and Worcester, two of the finest castles in England – Warwick and Kenilworth – and a selection of picturesque manor houses and stately homes. There is also one World Heritage Site and appropriately for an area renowned for its industrial heritage, it is an industrial site. The chief focal point of the Ironbridge Gorge is the world's first iron bridge but there are also a series of museums that illustrate the history of this unique place that helped to spawn the industries of Birmingham and the Black Country.

Useful addresses

The Ramblers' Association, 2nd Floor, Camelford House,
   87–90 Albert Embankment, London SE1 7TW
   Tel: 020 7339 8500

The National Trust, PO Box 39, Warrington WA5 7WD
   Tel: 0870 458 4000

English Heritage, Customer Services Department, PO Box
   569, Swindon SN2 2YP Tel: 0870 333 1181

Local Tourist Information Centres:

Bewdley 01299 404740
Birmingham 0121 202 5099
Bromsgrove 01527 831809
Coventry 024 7622 7264
Droitwich Spa 01905 774312
Dudley 01384 812830
Evesham 01386 446944
Ironbridge 01952 432166
Kenilworth 01926 748900
Leamington Spa 01926 742762
Lichfield 01543 412121
Merry Hill 01384 481141
Nuneaton 024 7638 4027
Redditch 01527 60806
Solihull 0121 704 0768
Stafford 01785 619619
Stratford-upon-Avon 0870 160 7930
Tamworth 01827 709581
Walsall 01922 625540
Warwick 01926 492212
Wolverhampton 01902 556110
Worcester 01905 726311

Public transport

For information about bus and train services either phone Traveline on 0870 608 2608 or contact the local tourist information centre

The Walks

The sketch maps are only a rough guide and you should always take with you an Ordnance Survey (O.S.) map. The best maps for walkers are the Explorer maps and the number and title of the relevant ones are given in the introductory information for each route.

Visiting historic sites

Some of the historic buildings and sites featured in the walks are open all the year round and are free to look round but most have restricted opening times and charge an entrance fee. In particular some English Heritage properties and most stately homes are closed during the winter months, approximately from the end of October to around Easter time. In order to avoid disappointment, it is always best to enquire about opening times by contacting either the individual site or the nearest tourist information centre. The relevant phone numbers are provided.

Walk map key

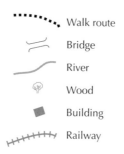

Walk route

Bridge

River

Wood

Building

Railway

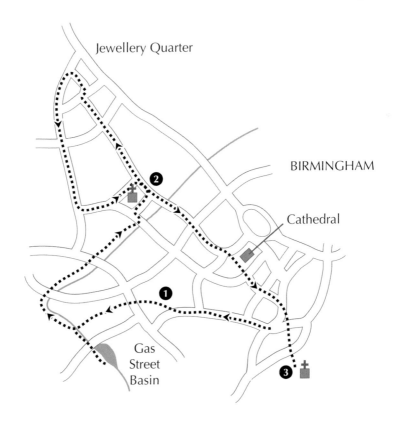

Jewellery Quarter

BIRMINGHAM

②

Cathedral

①

Gas
Street
Basin

③

WALK 1

Birmingham: City Centre, Canals and Jewellery Quarter

LENGTH:	7.2 km (4.5 miles)
TIME:	2 hours
TERRAIN:	Easy town walking with one stretch along canal towpaths
START/PARKING:	Birmingham, Victoria Square, GR SP066868. Car parks in Birmingham city centre
BUS/TRAIN:	Birmingham is easily reached by bus and train from all the local towns
REFRESHMENTS:	Plenty of pubs, cafes and restaurants in Birmingham
MAP:	O.S. Explorer 220 – Birmingham, or pick up a town map from the Tourist Information Centre

This fascinating walk through Birmingham's city centre and historic Jewellery Quarter is a varied mixture of old and new. It includes most of the city's imposing Victorian civic buildings, the exciting recent developments around Centenary Square and the International Convention Centre, a visit to Gas Street Basin – hub of the canal system for which Birmingham is renowned – and a canalside walk. The route also takes in the city's only remaining Georgian square, the early eighteenth-century cathedral and the well-known

Bullring, dominated by two very diverse structures – the rebuilt medieval St Martin's church and the striking twenty-first-century Selfridges building.

ⓘ Victoria Square is the hub of Britain's second city and around it are grouped most of the great civic buildings erected in the late nineteenth century when Birmingham was 'the workshop of the world'. The finest of these are the magnificent Council House, built in the 1870s in the Renaissance style, and the Town Hall, an imitation Roman temple which opened in 1834. A more recent and eye catching addition is a cascading fountain erected when the square was landscaped in the 1990s. Its official name is 'The River' but Brummies have nicknamed it – for obvious reasons – 'The Floosie in the Jacuzzi'.

Birmingham Town Hall

The nineteenth-century Council House in Victoria Square

In the smaller adjoining Chamberlain Square is the City Museum and Art Gallery, opened in 1885. Its clock tower is known as 'Big Brum'. The Chamberlain Fountain in the middle of the square was erected in honour of Joseph Chamberlain, the great Victorian civic leader and three times mayor in the 1870s who did much to improve the city.

❶ From Victoria Square pass between the Town Hall and Council House into Chamberlain Square. Walk through Paradise Forum and on across a bridge into Centenary Square and continue across the square to the International Convention Centre.

🛈 Centenary Square was laid out in 1989 to commemorate
Birmingham's centenary as a borough. The buildings around
it range from the 1920s to the 1990s. The Hall of Memory
– the city's war memorial – and Baskerville House were
built in the inter-war years. Adjacent to the latter is the
Repertory Theatre which dates from 1971. The impressive
International Convention Centre opened in 1991and as well
as hosting prestigious conferences of all kinds, it houses
Symphony Hall, widely regarded as one of the finest
concert halls in the world.

🚶 **After passing through the International Convention
Centre, cross a bridge over the canal and ahead is
Brindleyplace.**

🛈 The recent development of Brindleyplace is a mixture of
striking modern buildings in a variety of architectural styles.
They include offices, shops, restaurants, wine bars, coffee
shops and pubs. In addition a Victorian school has been
transformed into the Ikon Gallery, a contemporary art
gallery. Fountains and sculptures complete the scene and
the whole area has a pleasantly relaxed atmosphere.

A short distance to the left is Gas Street Basin, definitely
worth a brief detour. During the late eighteenth and
nineteenth centuries this was the hub of Birmingham's
canal network and the meeting place of two canal systems,
the Birmingham Canal Navigations and the Worcester
and Birmingham Canal. A seven-foot wide barrier, the
Worcester Bar, separated the canals and because of rivalry
between the companies, goods had to be hauled from
one canal to the other until agreement was reached and
a stop lock was constructed in 1815. In recent years the
area around the basin has been revitalised and is now an
attractive marina lined with pubs, restaurants, hotels, wine
bars and a mixture of old and new buildings.

(※) **The main route continues to the right alongside the canal, passing in front of the Sea Life Centre. After going up a ramp, turn right to cross the canal to the National Indoor Arena and in front of it, turn sharp left down steps – doubling back – and turn left under the bridge. Continue beside the Birmingham and Fazeley Canal, descending the Farmer's Bridge flight of locks, and keep by it as far as a sign for the Jewellery Quarter where the canal enters a tunnel. Climb steps to a road (Newhall Street) and turn left, passing the Assay Office on the right. Turn first right along Charlotte Street into St Paul's Square. ❷**

❶ St Paul's Square, lined by dignified eighteenth-century brick buildings and an oasis of calm amidst the bustle of the city, is Birmingham's only surviving Georgian square. In the centre is St Paul's church, built in the 1770s and formerly known as the 'Jewellers Church', because of its close links with the industry. Among the people who have worshipped here are the famous duo of Matthew Boulton and James Watt, creators of the steam engine. The square is the gateway to the Jewellery Quarter.

The jewellery trade has been based in this part of Birmingham for over 200 years and developed out of the manufacture of trinkets and toys. As the industry grew and became concentrated more and more within this small area, most of the gardens of the houses became built over and crammed with workshops. The Jewellery Quarter was at its height in the late nineteenth and early twentieth centuries and around 1910 over 30,000 people were employed here. After a period of decline, it has had a revival since the 1980s and has developed into more of a retail area, with over 100 jewellery shops. It has also become a popular and stylish residential area, with a number of apartments created either from new buildings or from the renovation of former workshops and warehouses.

Centenary Square

🚶 **The next part of the route is a circuit of the Quarter. Turn left across St Paul's churchyard and keep ahead along Caroline Street to a crossroads. Continue along Spencer Street and turn right by the Jewellers Arms into Hockley Street. Turn left into Branston Street and left again into Vyse Street, passing the Museum of the Jewellery Quarter.**

ℹ️ A visit to the Museum of the Jewellery Quarter is a fascinating experience. It is housed in a virtual time capsule, the workshops and offices of the former jewellery firm of Smith and Pepper which were abandoned just as they were when the firm closed down in 1981. You can see displays on the history of the jewellery industry and also watch skilled jewellers at work. Tel: 0121 554 3598

🚶 **Continue along Vyse Street to the crossroads by the Chamberlain Clock Tower and keep ahead along Frederick Street. On the right you pass the impressive Renaissance-**

style Argent Centre, a fine example of Jewellery Quarter architecture. Turn left into Graham Street, passing a Sikh temple, follow the road around a right bend and turn left along Brook Street to return to St Paul's Square. ❷

Turn right across the churchyard again and keep ahead along Ludgate Hill. Cross the footbridge over Great Charles Street Ringway and walk up Church Street to emerge into Colmore Row opposite the cathedral.

ℹ️ Birmingham Cathedral is a rare example of an English Baroque church and was built by Thomas Archer, a pupil of Sir Christopher Wren, in the early eighteenth century. It was originally a parish church and was raised to cathedral status when the diocese of Birmingham was created in 1905. Although small, it is a dignified building situated in an attractive setting and the interior is especially noted for the four stained glass windows designed by Sir Edward Burne-Jones, a native of the city.

Tel: 0121 262 1840

Brindleyplace, at the heart of Birmingham's revitalised canal network

⊛ **Walk across the cathedral churchyard and continue down Cherry Street to Corporation Street. Cross over, walk along Union Street and in front of Marks and Spencer, turn right into High Street. At the corner of High Street and New Street, keep ahead to the Bullring and descend steps to the right of Nelson's statue to St Martin's church. ❸**

ℹ Originally spelt the Bull Ring – now rechristened the Bullring as part of its new image – this characterful area was the heart of medieval Birmingham. Hideously rebuilt in the 1960s, it has now thankfully been redesigned in a more attractive and sympathetic manner. The most striking new building is Selfridges, a structure about which there are no half measures – you either love it or loathe it.

The Georgian St Paul's church, gateway to the Jewellery Quarter

Birmingham Cathedral

St Martin's is the mother church of Birmingham and there has been a church on this site since the thirteenth century. It has been restored several times and was comprehensively rebuilt in the 1880s but still retains some of the tombs of the De Bermingham family, the medieval lords of the manor.

Retrace your steps to the corner of High Street and New Street, turn left along New Street and follow it back to Victoria Square.

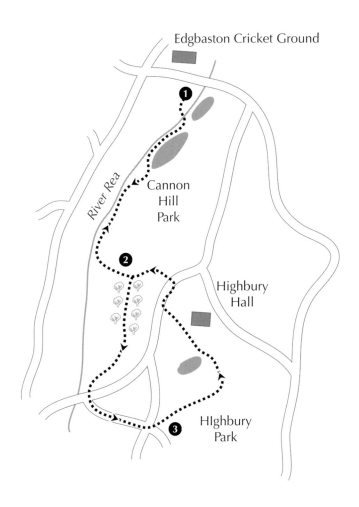

Edgbaston Cricket Ground

River Rea

Cannon
Hill
Park

Highbury
Hall

HIghbury
Park

WALK 2

Two Birmingham Parks: Cannon Hill and Highbury

LENGTH:	6.4 km (4 miles)
TIME:	2 hours
TERRAIN:	Gentle walking mostly on tarmac paths and tracks across parks
START/PARKING:	Cannon Hill Park, GR SP067841. The car park is opposite Edgbaston cricket ground
BUS/TRAIN:	Buses from Birmingham city centre
REFRESHMENTS:	Cafes in Cannon Hill Park, pub on the corner of Dad's Lane
MAP:	O.S. Explorer 220 – Birmingham

Although in the southern suburbs of Birmingham and scarcely more than 3.2 km (2 miles) from the city centre, this walk in the Rea valley is surprisingly rural – at times there is not a building in sight – and avoids roads almost entirely. It takes you across a large green wedge, making use of two almost adjacent parks linked by a strip of woodland and area of grassland. Apart from the parks, historic interest is provided by glimpses of Highbury Hall, home of Joseph Chamberlain, the nineteenth-century statesman and thrice Mayor of Birmingham.

Cannon Hill Park

⟨⚘⟩ ❶ **From the car park cross the bridge over the River Rea by the Midlands Arts Centre to enter Cannon Hill Park.**

ⓘ Cannon Hill is one of the city's most popular and colourful parks and comprises around 80 acres of formal parkland plus an adjoining 120 acres of meadow, wetland and woodland. The River Rea that runs along its western edge has always been something of a local joke; although Birmingham's major river it is no more than a small stream.

The park was formerly the estate of the Ryland family. In 1873 not only did the family donate it to the people of Birmingham but they also financed a landscaping programme which included the planting of ornamental gardens and the construction of pools. The Birmingham Nature Centre and Midlands Arts Centre are both situated within the park. Across the other side of the pool is a former inn, the Golden Lion, a half-timbered structure that dates from the seventeenth century. It previously stood in Deritend in the centre of Birmingham and was re-erected here in 1911 to avoid demolition.

Turn right onto a tarmac track along the right side of the pool and at a junction of paths near the end of the pool, turn left over a brick bridge. Immediately turn right onto a track, at a Rea Valley Walkway sign, and continue by the river on the right as far as a fork and signpost by a footbridge. Take the left hand path to a T-junction and

Rea Valley; in the suburbs of Birmingham and not a building in sight

turn left, in the Moseley direction, heading gently uphill towards Holders Lane Woods. At the top turn right ❷ – not along the tarmac path but onto a path that leads off into the trees and keeps roughly parallel with the tarmac track.

As you follow the path through the strip of woodland, gaps in the trees on the right reveal fine views over the Rea valley, with the tower of Birmingham University prominent on the skyline. Keep on the main path all the while, ignoring all side paths, and at a three-way fork, take the right hand path which joins a tarmac track. Continue along it and pass beside two barriers in quick succession to emerge onto a road in front of the Highbury pub.

Birmingham's river: the Rea near Cannon Hill Park

Holder's Lane Woods

Highbury Hall, home of Joesph Chamberlain the great municipal reformer

Turn right, almost immediately turn left by the pub and head uphill along Dad's Lane. At a road junction at the top, cross over Shutlock Lane to enter Highbury Park ❸ and continue along a wide, straight, tree-lined tarmac track.

❶ Highbury Park was the parkland surrounding Highbury Hall, the home of Joseph Chamberlain. As a statesman whose name is synonymous with Birmingham, it comes as something of a surprise to discover that he was not a Brummie but a Londoner and he named the house after the area of London where he previously lived. The hall was built in 1880 by JH Chamberlain (no relation), an architect who was heavily influenced by Ruskin. Nowadays it is a conference centre.

Joseph Chamberlain first came to the Midlands in 1854 to join the family screw manufacturing business and quickly immersed himself in local politics, rising through the ranks to become three times Mayor of Birmingham in the 1870s. Under his dynamic and forceful leadership Birmingham pioneered a number of civic improvements such as the provision of gas and water supplies, slum clearance and educational improvement. He also played a major role in the construction of Corporation Street – based on a Parisian boulevard – the building of the Council House and the founding of Birmingham University of which he was the first Chancellor. From local politics he went on to Westminster and served as a minister in both Liberal and Conservative governments.

🕃 **Take the first path on the left which curves left and at a left bend – just before reaching a narrow pool on the left – turn right onto a grassy path which heads gently uphill through the trees of Highbury Arboretum. Glimpses of the façade of Highbury Hall can be seen through the trees on the right, especially when they are not in leaf. At the top the path joins a tarmac track which bends left and passes beside a lodge onto a road.**

Keep ahead along Moor Green Lane and turn left into Holders Lane. Where the lane curves left, keep ahead along an enclosed tarmac track which later narrows to a path and passes along the edge of Holders Lane Woods. ❷ Here you pick up the outward route and retrace your steps to the start.

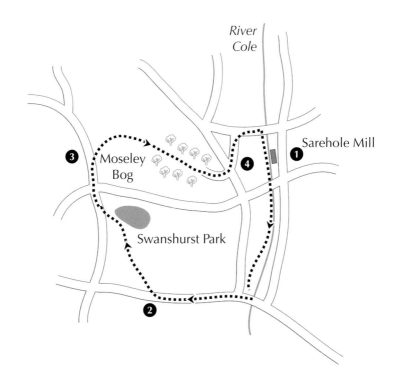

*River
Cole*

3

Moseley
Bog

1 Sarehole Mill

4

Swanshurst Park

2

WALK 3

Tolkien Country: Sarehole Mill and Moseley Bog

LENGTH:	4.8 km (3 miles)
TIME:	1.5 hours
TERRAIN:	Riverside paths, grassland and woodland
START/PARKING:	Birmingham, The Shire Country Park, Sarehole Mill, off Cole Bank Road on the borders of Moseley and Hall Green, GR SP099819
BUS/TRAIN:	Buses from Birmingham city centre
REFRESHMENTS:	Tearoom serving drinks and snacks at Sarehole Mill
MAP:	O.S. Explorer 220 – Birmingham

This is a walk with a strong Tolkien theme as it visits many places in the Cole valley on the south side of Birmingham associated with the author's childhood. Given the wilderness nature of parts of the route, especially in the dense woodland of Moseley Bog – real Hobbit country – it is difficult to believe that this is only a small rural enclave surrounded by suburban roads and houses.

🛈 Sarehole Mill was once one of many mills on the River Cole but is now the only survivor. This water-powered corn mill dates from the eighteenth century but there has been a mill on the site since the Middle Ages. After falling into

Sarehole Mill

disrepair, it was restored in the 1960s and opened as a museum.

Nowadays Sarehole Mill is principally noted for its close links with JRR Tolkien and in recognition of those links and the affection that he felt for the place and surrounding area when he was a small boy, Tolkien contributed to the mill's restoration fund. Between 1896 and 1900 the family lived in a house nearby and both Tolkien and his brother used to visit the mill and play in the adjoining meadows. The writer describes the miller and his son – frightening looking men covered in white dust – who used to chase the boys away from the mill. At the time the local area was still very rural: Moseley was little more than a country village and the city's suburbs did not extend out this far until after World War I. This area of the Cole valley is said to be the inspiration for The Shire, home to the Hobbits.

Tel: 0121 777 6612

❶ Leave the car park, cross Cole Bank Road and take the tarmac path opposite, called the John Morris Jones Walkway. The path heads through trees beside the River Cole to emerge onto a road. Turn right and on the corner of Brook Lane and Wake Green Road there are a few surviving post-war Birmingham prefabs.

These prefabs at the bottom end of Wake Green Road are rare survivals of the many that were hurriedly erected in Birmingham – and throughout the country – after 1945. They were a way of solving the desperate shortage of housing and building materials in post-war Britain and were originally intended only to have a short lifespan.

Keep ahead uphill along Brook Lane and over the brow Swanshurst Park appears on the right. Turn half-right, ❷ head diagonally across the grass and then bear right to follow a path across a rough grassy area towards trees. Continue by the left edge of the trees to a pool and turn left along a tarmac path beside it to a road. Turn right and at a crossroads keep ahead along Yardley Wood Road. Where you see a sign to Moseley Bog on the left hand side of the road, turn right over a stile onto a path, ❸ soon bearing right on joining a track.

The woodland of Moseley Bog is thought to be the inspiration for the Old Forest in the Lord of the Rings novels. Although only covering a small area (22 acres)

Moseley Bog – was this Tolkien's Old Forest?

and surrounded by suburban roads and houses, it is still
a place of mystery where the imagination can run riot.
The woodland is thick and some of the old trees can look
quite menacing. Parts of it can also be boggy after wet
weather. It is now preserved as a local nature reserve by
Birmingham City Council.

Where the track ends, keep ahead along a path through
the trees of Joy's Wood. On reaching a junction of paths
in a clearing, keep ahead, plunging into thick woodland.
Look out for steps on the left, descend them, keep by
a brook on the right, cross a plank footbridge and bear
right onto a broader path, still by the brook. It is on this
part of the walk that you really feel that you are in a
remote, boggy, ancient and rather spooky forest. Because
of the marshy ground, most of the walking is done on
boardwalks.

At a T-junction of boardwalks, turn right and shortly
– before reaching some steps – turn right to cross a plank
footbridge over the brook. Turn left, immediately follow

the path to the right uphill and turn left down steps
to emerge from the trees into suburban Birmingham.
Walk across grass to the end of a road, turn left and at
a T-junction, turn right into Pensby Close. At the next
T-junction turn left along Thirlmere Drive to another
T-junction and turn left again into Wake Green Road, ❹
passing number 264.

ℹ️ The house at 264 Wake Green Road was Tolkien's
childhood home from 1896 to 1900, years that he
considered the happiest of his life. It is now a private
residence.

🚶 Bear right along Gracewell Road – more like a country
lane – and at a T-junction, turn right into Green Road.
Follow it downhill to the ford over the Cole and in front
of it, turn right through a fence gap and walk along the
left edge of a meadow. In the corner of the meadow, a
footbridge on the left leads back into the car park.

The ford over the River Cole near Sarehole Mill

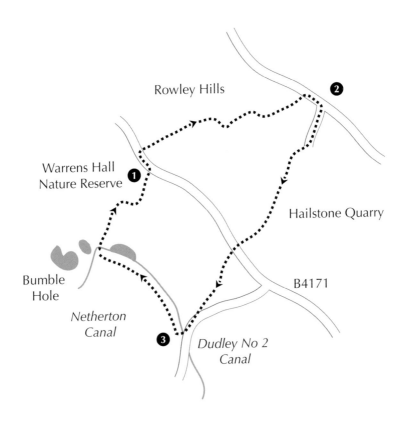

Rowley Hills

Warrens Hall
Nature Reserve ❶

Hailstone Quarry

Bumble
Hole

*Netherton
Canal*

❸

B4171

*Dudley No 2
Canal*

WALK 4

Rowley Hills and Bumble Hole

LENGTH:	4.8 km (3 miles)
TIME:	1.5 hours
TERRAIN:	Easy climb and descent followed by a canal towpath
START/PARKING:	Warrens Hall Nature Reserve, Rowley Regis, off B4171 between Blackheath and Dudley, GR SO962881
BUS/TRAIN:	Buses from Dudley and Halesowen
REFRESHMENTS:	Pubs at the top of the Rowley Hills, pub at Springfield, pubs at Bumble Hole and tearoom at Bumble Hole Visitor Centre
MAP:	O.S. Explorer 219 – Wolverhampton & Dudley

The main part of the walk is over Turner's Hill, one of the two Rowley Hills that rise to a height of 267 m (876 feet) above the Black Country and provide a welcome oasis of greenery as well as a succession of fine views. After descending from the hill, the route continues along the Dudley No 2 Canal to the fascinating conservation area of Bumble Hole, formerly a highly industrialised area but now a green and quiet nature reserve used for recreation. From there it is a short walk back to the start.

ⓘ Although it is difficult to envisage, Warrens Hall Local
Nature Reserve was once the busy, dirty and noisy site
of coal mines, blast furnaces, iron works, brick kilns and
factories, built on land owned by the earls of Dudley. Now
it has been landscaped to create a green and attractive
haven for wildlife and there is little to remind visitors of
this former industrial activity apart from some colliery spoil
tips.

🚶 ❶ **Leave the car park and turn left along the B4171. Just
after passing Banklands Road on the left, turn right onto
a tarmac path which heads uphill over the Rowley Hills.
About 183 m (200 yards) after passing to the right of a
pool, turn right to continue uphill along another tarmac
path.**

**Where the path bends left, turn right and at a post,
turn left onto an uphill path, passing through a belt of
trees. Bear left across rough grassland, making for a wide
gap in the trees by a disused quarry, bear right around
the edge of the quarry and continue in a roughly straight**

Rowley Hills

Entrance to the Netherton Tunnel near Bumble Hole

line across Dudley golf course, looking out for a series of
marker posts. On the far side, keep ahead through trees
to emerge onto Oakham Road near the top of Turner's
Hill.

🛈 The Rowley Hills comprise two summits, Turner's Hill and
the adjacent Darby's Hill. From them the views extend
across the Black Country to the Clent Hills, Barr Beacon
and Cannock Chase. In the past the hills were extensively
quarried for their durable, dark grey dolerite rock, known
locally as Rowley Rag and much used throughout the
Midlands for kerbstones and road surfaces. On the descent
you pass along the edge of the vast Hailstone Quarry.

🚶 Turn right and take the first lane on the right, ❷ passing
between two pubs, the Wheatsheaf on the right and
the Rowley Olympic on the left. After passing beside a
barrier, look out for a stile on the right which admits you
to the golf course again. Keep ahead to a yellow-topped

Canal bridges and Cobb's Engine House, relics of former industrial activity at Bumble Hole

post and beyond that you pick up a clear path that heads downhill along the left edge of the course beside the boundary fence of the Hailstone Quarry to a stile.

Climb it, continue downhill by a fence on the right, climb a stile, keep ahead and climb another stile at the bottom. Turn left along a tarmac track which bends right by Springfield Social Club to emerge onto the B4171 in Springfield opposite the Hailstone pub. Cross the main road, walk along the short stretch of road opposite (Springfield Close) and at a public footpath sign, turn left onto a tarmac path. At a fork take the left hand path and follow it around a right bend. Cross the end of a road and continue downhill along an enclosed tarmac path to a road.

Turn right down to a canal bridge and after crossing it, turn sharp left down steps to the towpath of the Dudley No 2 Canal. ❸ Turn left under the bridge and follow the towpath to the large canal basin at Bumble Hole.

ⓘ Like the adjoining Warrens Hall, the canal basin at Bumble Hole is a former busy mining and manufacturing area now transformed into an attractive nature reserve. It is situated at the junction of two canals – Netherton and Dudley No 2 – and once served the local coal mines. Unlike Warrens Hall, it has preserved more of its industrial heritage and the combination of picturesque cast iron bridges, marina, canal junction and pools, overlooked by Cobb's Engine House, creates an exceptionally attractive and atmospheric industrial environment, a reminder of the past heyday of the Black Country. As a reflection of this there is a Visitor Centre beside the canal. Tel: 01384 814 100

A short distance along the Netherton Canal is the entrance to the Netherton Tunnel, 2768 m (3027 feet) long. It was constructed in the 1850s and was the last great tunnel of the canal era. Nearby is Cobb's Engine House, named after a local farmer, which formerly housed a Watt Beam Engine, used to pump water out of the local deep mines which were prone to regular flooding. It was built in 1831 and ceased working in 1928.

🏃 **Turn right over the iron bridge – the one nearest the canal not the brick bridge – pass under the next bridge towards the entrance to the Netherton Tunnel and just after passing under a brick bridge, turn right up a flight of steps. Turn left at the top, pass to the left of Cobb's Engine House and take the uphill path ahead. On reaching a well-surfaced path, turn right and cross a footbridge over an outlet stream.**

The path curves left along the right side of a pool to a T-junction. Turn left along a tarmac path to return to the start.

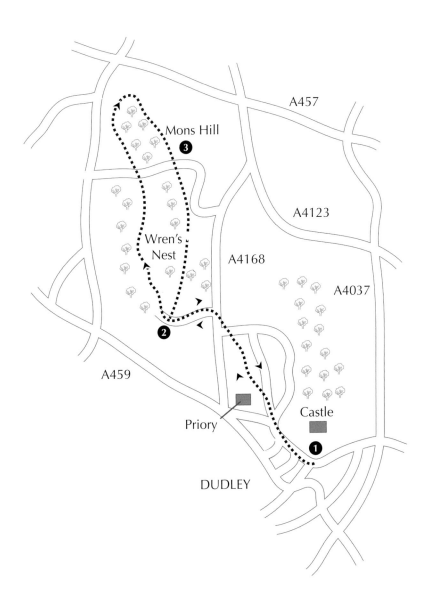

A457

Mons Hill
❸

A4123

Wren's
Nest

A4168

A4037

❷

A459

Priory

Castle

❶

DUDLEY

WALK 5

Dudley and Wren's Nest

LENGTH:	6.4 km (4 miles)
TIME:	2 hours
TERRAIN:	Short stretches of road walking, tarmac paths across a park and woodland tracks; three flights of steps
START/PARKING:	Dudley, in the town centre at the junction of Castle Hill, Castle Street and The Broadway, GR SO946905. Pay car parks in the centre of Dudley
BUS/TRAIN:	Buses from Birmingham, Wolverhampton and all the surrounding towns
REFRESHMENTS:	Pubs and cafes at Dudley, pub between Wren's Nest and Mons Hill
MAP:	O.S. Explorer 219 – Wolverhampton & Dudley

It is surprising how quickly you escape from the busy town centre and suburban roads of Dudley first into attractive parkland and then through the wooded and hilly terrain of the Wren's Nest National Nature Reserve. As well as the fine woodland, this is an area of unique geological interest and from several points there are extensive and impressive views over the Black Country.

ⓘ Most Black Country towns are largely the creation of
the Industrial Revolution but the hilltop town of Dudley
has a much longer history, as its castle and priory ruins
indicate. At the time that Domesday Book was compiled
on the orders of William the Conqueror in 1086, it was
the administrative centre of a large estate which included
what was then a small and insignificant village called
Birmingham.

Dudley Castle, stronghold of the medieval Lords of
Dudley, was founded in the eleventh century shortly after
the Norman Conquest. It is dominated by its imposing
keep, erected during a fourteenth-century rebuilding. Many
of the other buildings date from the Tudor period when
the current owner John Dudley, Earl of Northumberland,
reconstructed the castle in order to make it a more modern
and comfortable residence. Its defences were destroyed
after the Civil War and it subsequently fell into ruin. The
Dudley family later moved first to Himley Hall and then on
to Witley Court. Since the 1930s the grounds have housed
a zoo. Tel: 01384 215316

🚶 **❶ Facing the castle, turn left down The Broadway to
Priory Park and the ruins of Dudley Priory. Bear right
into Paganel Drive but almost immediately turn left onto
a tarmac path by the priory.**

ⓘ The small Cluniac priory of St James was founded in the
twelfth century by Gervase Paganel, Lord of Dudley and
was dissolved by Henry VIII in 1536. Not much is left
except for parts of the church, especially the west front,
and the foundations of some of the domestic buildings
around the cloister.

🚶 **The path curves right and heads across Priory Park
towards a large house, Priory Hall, built in 1825 and
now used by the local council. Bear right onto a path**

which passes in front of the house, continue through a
rose garden and at a fork, take the right hand path along
the right edge of the park, later bearing left across it to
emerge onto a road.

Turn left to a junction, turn right along the main road
and take the first road on the left (Cedar Road). Where
the road ends, continue uphill along a tarmac path and
at a T-junction, turn right ❷ beside a gate to enter the
Wren's Nest Nature Reserve. Walk along a path through
trees and turn left when you see a flight of steps. At the

Priory ruins at Dudley

Wren's Nest, formerly a quarry and now a nature reserve

top, turn right along a ridge top path. From here there are extensive views to the right over Dudley, with the castle keep standing out prominently, and across much of the Black Country towards the buildings in the centre of Birmingham on the skyline. Keep ahead along the main path, turn left up the next flight of steps and turn right to walk along a parallel path to reach a viewing platform over the ripple beds.

ⓘ Centuries of quarrying activities on the limestone hills of Wren's Nest and the adjoining Mons Hill only ceased in the 1920s, by which time they had become honeycombed with caves and underground passages. The limestone served a variety of purposes: as building material and mortar – both the castle and priory at Dudley were constructed from it – agricultural fertiliser and later for use in the rapidly expanding iron industries of the Black Country.

The ripple marks can be seen on the rocks at Wren's Nest

Nowadays Wren's Nest is a National Nature Reserve, noted for its geological importance and in particular for its unique and extensive collection of fossils preserved in the limestone. Although virtually impossible to envisage, these creatures inhabited the coral reefs and tropical seas that covered this area around 420 million years ago. The fossilised remains of one such creature cropped up so frequently that it was nicknamed the 'Dudley Bug'. From the viewing platform, the ripple marks can clearly be seen on the rocks below, the result of the action of the waves all those millions of years ago.

View over the Black Country from Wren's Nest

ⓧ Turn left, descend the steps for a closer look at the ripple beds and coral reefs and at the bottom, turn right along a path which emerges via a barrier onto a road by the Caves pub. Cross over and pass beside another barrier to do a circuit of the adjoining woodland of Mons Hill. Take the path ahead and after 400 m (0.25 mile), look out for where a winding path leads off to the right. At a T-junction, turn right up steps to continue along the other side of the hill, later descending to the road crossed earlier.

Turn left downhill ❸ and turn right over a stile to re-enter Wren's Nest. Continue through woodland along the bottom edge of the hill, negotiating a series of stiles and barriers, to eventually emerge onto a tarmac path. Turn left, here rejoining the outer route, and retrace your steps through Priory Park back to Dudley town centre.

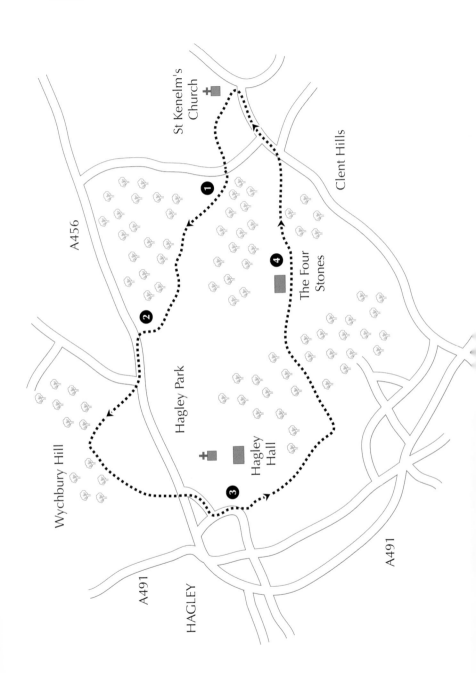

St Kenelm's Church

Clent Hills

A456

The Four Stones

Hagley Park

Wychbury Hill

Hagley Hall

HAGLEY

A491

A491

WALK 6

Clent Hills and Hagley Hall

LENGTH:	8 km (5 miles)
TIME:	2.5 hours
TERRAIN:	Easy to follow paths and tracks across fields and through woodland, two steady climbs
START/PARKING:	Clent Hills Country Park, Nimmings Wood car park, follow signs to Clent Hills from A456 between Halesowen and Hagley, GR SO939808
BUS/TRAIN:	Buses from Birmingham and Kidderminster pass through Hagley from where the walk could be picked up at point 2
REFRESHMENTS:	Café at Nimmings Wood car park
MAP:	O.S. Explorer 219 – Wolverhampton & Dudley

Generations of Brummies and Black Country people have flocked to the 'bald and breezy heights' of the Clent Hills on fine weekends and bank holidays and it is easy to see why. The series of well-wooded slopes make fine walking country and the views from the higher points on the route – Wychbury Hill and Clent Hill – are superb, extensive and contrasting, ranging from the Wrekin and Clee Hills in Shropshire to the tower blocks of the Black Country.

Wychbury Hill

❶ Begin by going down the fence-lined, zigzag path to the right of the visitor centre to a kissing gate. Go through, walk gently downhill across a field, go through another kissing gate and continue through a small wooded area. Go through a kissing gate on the far side, keep ahead across a field towards woodland and climb a stile on the edge of the trees.

Bear left to climb another stile and continue diagonally across a field, looking out for a stile which admits you to Hagley Wood. Head gently downhill through the wood, turn left to go through a gap and walk along the right edge of a field. At a hedge corner, turn right to pick up and continue along an enclosed track. About 91 m (100 yards) before reaching a farm, look out for a waymarked stile on the right. Climb it, walk across a field and climb a stile onto the busy A456. ❷ Turn left – there is a footpath – and at a traffic island, carefully cross onto the other side. A few yards to the left of Wassell Grove Lane, head down through a gap in the hedge to a stile, climb it and continue along the right edge of a field, climbing gently towards the top of Wychbury Hill.

Before reaching the prominent obelisk seen ahead, the path bears right to keep along the field edge to a stile on the edge of woodland. Do not climb it but turn left along the left edge of the trees to another stile.

ⓘ Wychbury Hill rises to a height of 224 m (734 feet) and is the site of an Iron Age fort, the earthworks of which are hidden by the trees that crown the summit. The obelisk was one of the follies erected by the Lyttleton family of Hagley Hall in the eighteenth century.

ⓧ Climb the stile and continue down to a gate. Go through, climb a stile beside another gate and continue down an enclosed track – it later becomes a tarmac lane – passing a row of cottages back to the A456. Cross over, turn right and take the first road on the left (School Lane). Follow the road around a right bend to a T-junction and turn left to reach another T-junction by the entrance to Hagley Hall. ❸

ⓘ Hagley Hall is a grand example of a large eighteenth-century country house enclosed within a contemporary landscaped park. One of the last of the great Palladian houses in England, it was designed by Sanderson Miller for the 1st Lord Lyttleton and built in the 1750s. After being badly damaged by an extensive fire in 1925 and thought to be beyond repair, it was subsequently restored to its previous glory. The rooms contain a fine collection of eighteenth-century paintings and furniture.

Nearby is the medieval church, heavily restored in the Victorian era. The park was landscaped at around the same time as the house was built and scattered throughout it are a number of follies. These include the obelisk on Wychbury Hill (already seen), a sham ruined castle, an imitation Classical temple and the Four Stones, a mock mini-Stonehenge on the summit of Clent Hill, which is passed shortly. Tel: 01562 882408

At the T-junction, keep ahead along an enclosed path, now on the North Worcestershire Path, and after passing beside a barrier, glimpses of Hagley Hall can be seen through the trees on the left. Pass beside another barrier and the path bears slightly left and heads gently uphill under an avenue of trees to a crossways. Turn left onto an enclosed uphill track, bear left onto another track – following North Worcestershire Path signs all the time – and look out for where a waymark directs you to turn right. Continue uphill along a tree-lined path, go through a gate, turn left and at a fork immediately ahead, take the right hand uphill path. Continue more steeply up the wooded slopes, keeping ahead at all path junctions, and eventually you emerge from the trees. Head up to the

The façade of Hagley Hall

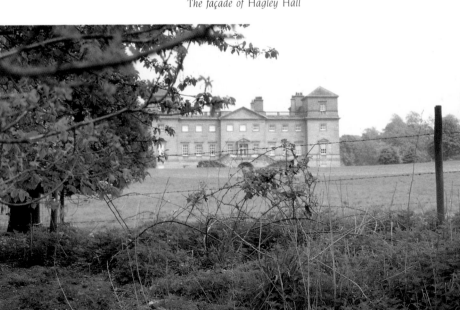

The four stones, an eighteenth-century folly on the summit of the Clent Hills

circle of trees that crown the summit of Clent Hill and bear left along the edge of these trees to the Four Stones. ❹

ⓘ They may look authentic but the Four Stones are a folly. They were placed here in the eighteenth century by Lord Lyttleton, builder of Hagley Hall, and his friend William Shenstone, a poet who lived nearby, in order to 'improve' the view of the hills.

Clent is the second highest point on the hills, 304 m high (997 feet), and gives its name to the whole range, probably because it is the most accessible and popular of the hills. The views from here are superb, extending from the edge of the Black Country across a large area of the Midlands to the outlines of the distant Wrekin and the Abberley, Clee and Malvern hills.

The small church of St Kenelm's, nestling below the Clent Hills

🚶 Continue past the Four Stones on a broad ridge path, re-entering woodland, and at a fork take the right hand path which descends quite steeply to a lane. Turn left, head downhill to St Kenelm's church and at a public footpath sign, turn left through a lych gate into the churchyard.

ℹ This little sandstone church stands on the site of the alleged martyrdom of St Kenelm, a legendary ninth-century boy king of Mercia murdered on the orders of his sister. A spring in the churchyard is supposed to mark the spot where this foul deed took place. Although much restored, the church still retains some original Norman work in the nave and chancel and has a Tudor south porch.

🚶 Turn left onto a tarmac path in front of the church, look out for a path which leads off from it to the right, go through a gap in the trees and keep ahead across grass to a kissing gate. Go through, bear slightly left across a field to a waymarked post where you go through a gap in a line of trees and continue across the next field to a stile.

Climb it, keep ahead to climb another one and turn left along a tree-lined, uphill path. Bear right and continue uphill across a field, making for the right hand edge of the prominent group of trees in front. Climb a stile onto a lane and the car park is ahead.

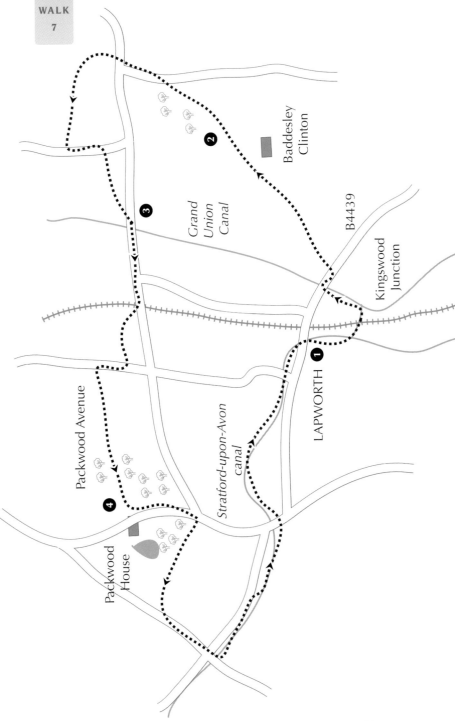

Baddesley
Clinton

2

Grand
Union
Canal

3

B4439

Kingswood
Junction

LAPWORTH

1

Packwood Avenue

Stratford-upon-Avon
canal

4

Packwood
House

WALK 7

Baddesley Clinton and Packwood House

LENGTH:	12.1 km (7.5 miles)
TIME:	4 hours
TERRAIN:	Mostly flat walking across fields and parkland plus canal towpaths
START/PARKING:	Lapworth, picnic area by the Stratford-upon-Avon Canal at Kingswood Junction, from the B4439 turn down Brome Hall Road and the car park and picnic area is on the left, GR SP186710
BUS/TRAIN:	Infrequent buses from Solihull and Warwick
REFRESHMENTS:	Pub at Lapworth, cafés at both Baddesley Clinton and Packwood House
MAP:	O.S. Explorer 220 – Birmingham and O.S. Explorer 221 – Coventry & Warwick

The route passes two contrasting manor houses, one late medieval and the other Tudor. Both are National Trust properties and are in delightful locations in the heart of the Warwickshire countryside. There is also a canal theme to this walk. It starts at a canal junction, takes in two stretches of canal and the last 2.4 km (1.5 miles) follows the towpath of the Stratford-upon-Avon Canal down the Lapworth flight of locks by which the canal drops from the Birmingham plateau to the Avon valley.

ⓘ The canal basin at Kingswood Junction is an attractive
spot with a marina, old canalside cottages and several
picturesque bridges. Nearby the Grand Union and Stratford-
upon-Avon canals run parallel for a short distance and a
spur, appropriately called the Lapworth Link, enables boats
to transfer from one to the other.

🚶 ❶ **Start by walking down to the canal and turn right
onto the towpath of the Stratford-upon-Avon Canal. Turn
left to cross bridge 36 and continue by the Lapworth
Link. Cross another bridge, turn left down steps and keep
along the canal, passing under a railway bridge. Turn left
to cross the next bridge (number 37) – here joining the
Grand Union Canal – and continue along its towpath to
the first bridge (number 65).**

**Go up steps to the road, turn right over the bridge,
pass the Navigation pub and at a public footpath sign,
turn left along a track, passing to the left of a house. Go
through a kissing gate, keep ahead and bear right to go
through a gate, Keep in the same direction across a field,
making for the far right corner where you go through
another kissing gate. Walk along the right field edge and
in the corner cross a brook and go through a kissing
gate, here entering the parkland of Baddesley Clinton.**

**Continue along the right field edge and where the
fence on the right turns right, keep ahead across the
parkland and go through a kissing gate onto a tarmac
drive. ❷ The route continues to the left but you turn
right in order to visit Baddesley Clinton.**

ⓘ Enclosed by a moat and surrounded by wooded parkland,
Baddesley Clinton is everyone's idea of how a medieval
English manor house should look. It was built in the
fifteenth century and has changed little since the 1630s.
Throughout its history it has been owned by just two
families, first the Bromes and later the Ferrers. At the

Reformation the Ferrers remained staunchly loyal to the Roman Catholic faith and gave refuge to Jesuit priests during the persecution of Elizabeth I's reign, as the several priest's hiding places indicate.

A tour of the house includes the family rooms, many noted for their portraits and fine panelling, the medieval kitchen, library and nineteenth-century chapel. Afterwards it is pleasant to take a relaxing stroll around the walled garden, woodland and lake. Tel: 01564 783294

Return to the kissing gate where you joined the tarmac drive ❷ and about 18 m (20 yards) beyond it, look out for a waymarked kissing gate on the right. Go through and walk along a narrow, winding enclosed path which continues along the right inside edge of woodland to a stile. Climb it, cross a plank footbridge and turn right onto another enclosed path, going through two kissing gates to reach a lane.

Turn left, turn right at a T-junction and where the road curves right, turn left along the drive to Convent Farm. Where the tarmac drive ends, keep ahead to climb two stiles and after the second one, turn left across the field to climb another one. Walk along an enclosed path and after climbing the next stile, the path becomes waterlogged for about 91 m (100 yards). This section is also likely to be overgrown but conditions do improve and the path finally emerges via a gate onto a lane.

Turn left and after about 274 m (300 yards) turn right, at a public footpath sign, and walk along the right edge of a field. Go through a kissing gate, bear left across two fields and go through a kissing gate onto a road. ❸ Turn right over a canal bridge, continue along the road and immediately after crossing a railway bridge, turn right, at a public footpath sign, onto a tarmac hedge-lined track. In front of the gates to a house, bear right along an enclosed path and after going through a kissing gate, the

The moated manor house of Baddesley Clinton

path curves left to a gate. Go through, cross a tarmac drive and go through a kissing gate opposite. Walk along the left field edge and go through another kissing gate onto a road.

Turn right and at a National Trust sign for Packwood Avenue, turn left through a kissing gate and walk along the straight tree-lined avenue. After going through two gates in quick succession, keep ahead towards the house, go through another gate, descend steps and head across grass to the road in front of Packwood House. ❹

ⓘ Packwood House is a Tudor manor house, built about a century after Baddesley Clinton in the 1560s. It was extended in the late seventeenth century. Inside there are many items of rare seventeenth- and eighteenth-century furniture, ornaments and tapestries but in many ways the most remarkable feature is to be found outside. This is the seventeenth-century Yew Garden at the side of the house, a collection of clipped yews that is said to represent the Sermon on the Mount. There are also flower gardens and the house is set amidst attractive parkland that includes a lakeside walk. Tel: 01564 783294

🚶 **Turn left and at a public footpath sign by a road junction, turn right up steps, go through a gate and walk along the right edge of a grassy area, passing to the right of a house. Continue along a path by woodland on the right,**

Packwood House

The Lapworth flight of locks on the Stratford-upon-Avon canal

go through a gate and keep ahead to a stile. Climb it and as you walk along the left edge of the parkland adjoining Packwood House, following a series of footpath posts, there is a glorious view to the right of the lake and house.

Climb a stile onto a lane, turn left and at a crossroads turn right along the B4439. Turn left through a gap at the end of a hedge and turn left again onto the towpath of the Stratford Canal. Follow it down the Lapworth flight of locks, crossing and recrossing the canal three times. After passing under bridge 35 you return to the start at Kingswood Junction.

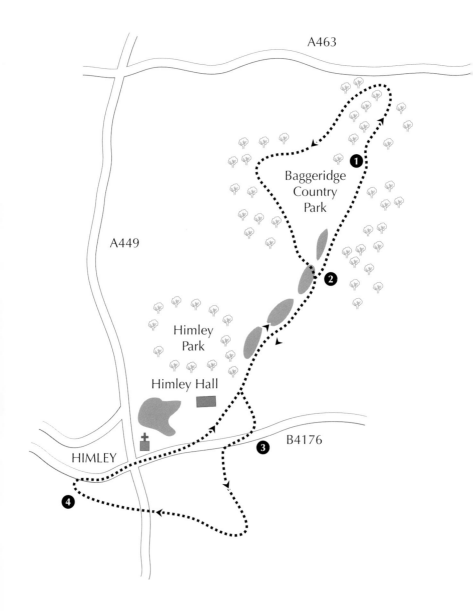

WALK 8

Two Adjacent Parks:
Baggeridge and Himley

DISTANCE:	9.7 km (6 miles)
TIME:	3 hours
TERRAIN:	Well-signed paths and tracks mostly across parkland and through woodland, one stretch along a disused railway track
START/PARKING:	Baggeridge Country Park Visitor Centre, entrance at Gospel End Village on the A463 between the A449 and Sedgley, GR SO898930
BUS/TRAIN:	Buses from Wolverhampton pass the entrance to Baggeridge Country Park
REFRESHMENTS:	Cafés at both Baggeridge Country Park and Himley Park
MAP:	O.S. Explorer 219 – Wolverhampton & Dudley

Parts of these peaceful, well-wooded and beautiful parklands on the western fringes of the Black Country were once busy, noisy and smoky industrial areas, so much so that the Earls of Dudley moved from their home at Himley Hall to a new residence in rural Worcestershire. Now the industries and coal mines have gone and formerly ugly and derelict sites have been reclaimed by nature and converted into popular recreational areas.

Gospel End Common, an area of Heathland on the edge of the Black Country

ⓘ The present Baggeridge Country Park was originally part of the Himley Estate of the Ward family, the Earls of Dudley. The southern half formed part of the landscaped parkland surrounding Himley Hall but from the late nineteenth century onwards, the northern half was extensively mined. After the colliery closed in 1968, the area was bought by the local council and years of careful and skilful landscaping transformed it into the present country park which opened in 1983. The park comprises an attractive mixture of woodland, heathland, meadows, streams and pools. Tel: 01902 882605

🚶 ❶ **Walk back along the drive towards the entrance and at a sign to Gospel End Common, turn left onto a path. Pass a waymarked post, climb a stile, cross a track and climb another stile opposite.**

Turn left along a hedge-lined track, enjoying fine views across the surrounding countryside on both sides. Soon after entering a belt of woodland the track descends and emerges from the trees to reach a crossways. Turn left to re-enter woodland and continue first along the left inside edge of the trees and later through Baggeridge Wood.

The track descends gently and curves left to a stile. Climb it, turn right down steps, cross a footbridge over a stream and turn right onto a track that keeps by the left edge of the stream. ❷

The way now continues along the left edge of a series of pools. First comes Spring Pool followed by Island Pool. After turning right around the end of the latter to a footpath sign to Himley Hall, bear left and go through a kissing gate. Here you leave Baggeridge Country Park and enter the neighbouring Himley Park. Continue along a tree-lined tarmac track, passing to the left of Rock Pool, to a T-junction by Himley Hall.

❶ The grand and dignified eighteenth-century mansion of Himley Hall was built to replace the medieval manor house on the site that the Earl of Dudley decided to demolish in 1740. During the process the original village of Himley was relocated, a new church was built in 1764 and the parkland surrounding the hall was landscaped by Capability Brown.

The Wards had moved to Himley from their castle at Dudley to escape from the noise and smoke of the Black Country. When industry later encroached here, they left Himley around the middle of the nineteenth century to seek rural tranquillity, this time to Witley Court in Worcestershire. Himley was not entirely abandoned as financial problems forced the family to sell Witley in 1920 and they returned to Himley. During the inter-war years the house became renowned for its glittering social occasions and was regularly visited by the Prince of Wales – later Edward VIII.

After World War II the hall was sold to the National Coal Board for offices and later it was purchased by Dudley Council. It is now used for all kinds of conferences, exhibitions and displays and can be hired for both public and private functions. Tel: 01384 817817

⊗ At the T-junction turn left and walk along the drive to the main vehicle entrance to the park. ❸ Turn right along the road and at a public footpath sign, turn left along a wide enclosed track. After passing a farm, keep ahead along a narrower track, go through a gate and continue to a disused railway bridge. In front of the bridge turn right beside a barrier, head up an embankment and at the top, turn right along a straight track.

ⓘ This is the track of a former railway that was built in 1912 to serve the rural area to the west of the Black Country. It was never very successful; the passenger service ceased as early as 1922 and the line finally closed down in 1965. Since then it has been converted into the Kingswinford Railway Path, a 8.9 km (5.5 miles) long footpath and cycleway.

⊗ Keep along the pleasantly tree-lined track for about 1.2 km (0.75 mile), crossing a road bridge. Just after crossing another bridge, turn sharp left down steps. ❹ At the bottom, turn sharp left along a track, pass under the bridge and follow the track through a gate and onto a

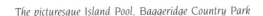

The picturesque Island Pool, Baggeridge Country Park

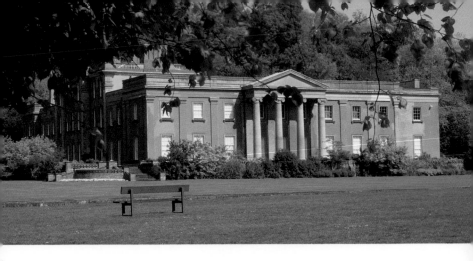

Himley Hall

road. Cross over and turn right – there is a footpath – to a crossroads and traffic lights.

Keep ahead, passing to the right of Himley's eighteenth-century church, and where the road bears slightly right, keep ahead through gates to re-enter Himley Park. Walk along a broad tree-lined drive towards the hall and after passing beside a barrier and through a parking area, bear left. Turn right beside Ward House and by a stream on the left, here rejoining the outward route, and follow the track alongside the succession of pools to where you earlier crossed the footbridge over the stream. ❷

Do not cross the footbridge but keep ahead uphill to a crossways and turn left beside Lower Wishing Pool. Head uphill above the pool and continue along the main well-surfaced track, following signs to Car Park. Almost all paths will bring you back to the visitor centre but for a quick and easy return follow the path around first a left curve, then a right curve and after another left curve – and just in front of a barrier for the car park – turn left along the right edge of an open grassy area fringed by mounds and bumps, the outlines of former waste tips. The path leads back to the start.

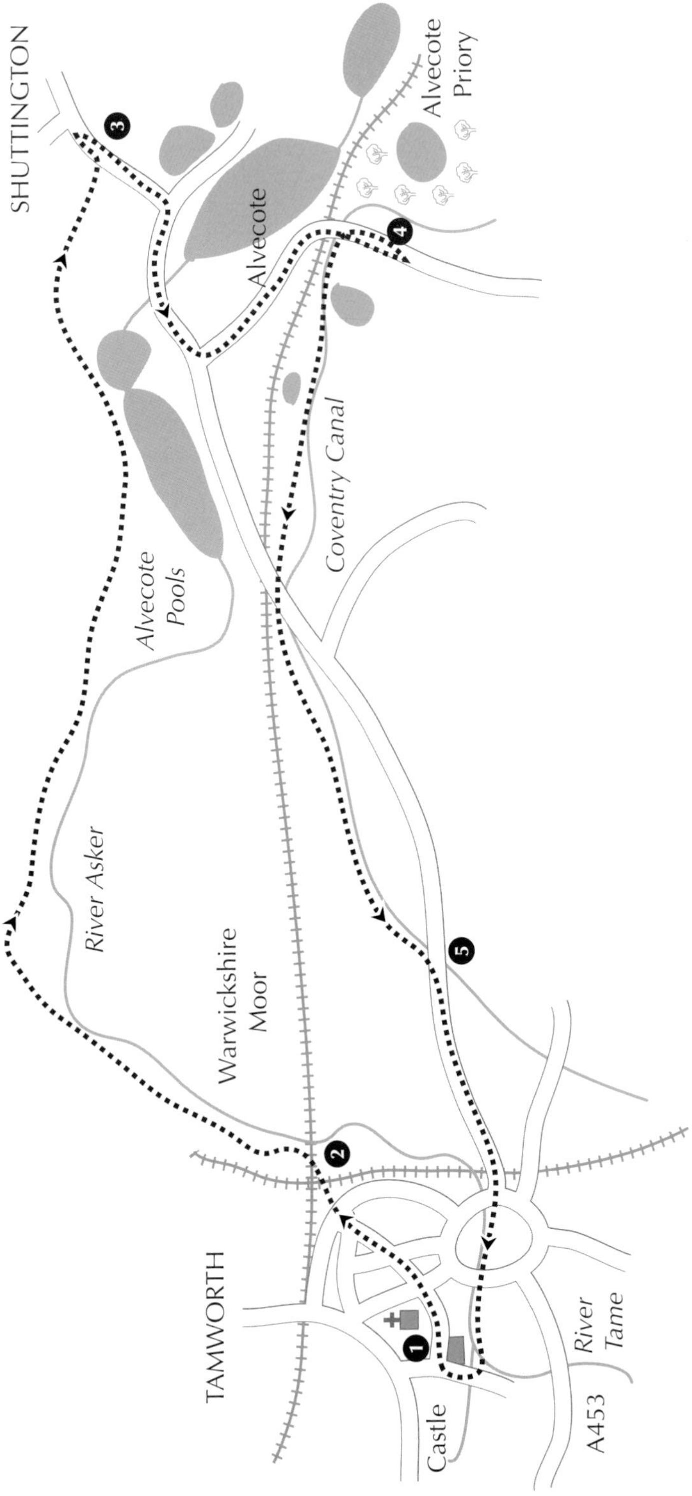
SHUTTINGTON
Alvecote
Alvecote Priory
Alvecote Pools
Coventry Canal
River Asker
Warwickshire Moor
TAMWORTH
Castle
River Tame
A453
1
2
3
4
5

WALK 9

Tamworth, River Anker and the Coventry Canal

LENGTH:	12.9 km (8 miles)
TIME:	4 hours
TERRAIN:	Flat walking on field and riverside paths, some of which may be muddy after rain, plus a canal towpath; also some road walking
START/PARKING:	Tamworth, in front of the Town Hall, GR SK206040. Plenty of pay car parks in the centre of Tamworth
BUS/TRAIN:	Buses from Birmingham, Lichfield, Stafford and Nuneaton; trains from Birmingham, Derby, Stafford and Nuneaton
REFRESHMENTS:	Pubs and cafes at Tamworth, pub at Shuttington, several pubs beside the Coventry Canal
MAP:	O.S. Explorer 232 – Nuneaton & Tamworth

From the busy town centre of Tamworth the route quickly and easily emerges into the pleasant countryside of the Anker valley on the Staffordshire-Warwickshire border and there are a series of extensive views over the flat expanses of Warwickshire Moor. The nature reserve of Alvecote Pools is at the approximate half-way stage and the return leg is mostly beside the Coventry Canal, with a final riverside stretch.

ⓘ In the eighth century Tamworth was the capital of Mercia, the seat of power of Offa the Great, the Mercian king who is best known for constructing the dyke to mark the boundary between his kingdom and Wales. The restored castle and imposing church both illustrate the former importance of the town.

Tamworth Castle was built by the Normans in the late eleventh century on the site of a tenth-century Saxon stronghold and the striking polygonal shell keep was constructed in the 1180s. Over the years it has been repeatedly rebuilt, altered and modernised and the varied buildings grouped around the courtyard date from the Middle Ages to the nineteenth century. A tour takes you through the whole range of the castle's history, including medieval dungeons, a fifteenth-century great hall and a series of Victorian rooms.

Tel: 01827 709626

The nearby church is a grand and spacious town church mainly dating from the fourteenth and fifteenth centuries built on the site of several earlier predecessors. Some impressive Norman arches remain from one of these. The massive central tower has a unique double spiral staircase.

The walk starts by the town hall, built at the beginning of the eighteenth century by Thomas Guy, founder of Guy's Hospital in London. The space beneath was a market. In front of it is a statue of the renowned nineteenth-century Prime Minister Sir Robert Peel, MP for Tamworth and founder of the Metropolitan Police Force.

⚸ ❶ Start by the Town Hall and walk eastwards along Market Street and George Street. Where the pedestrianised section ends, continue along Victoria

Road and keep ahead to cross a main road at a traffic roundabout near the railway station. Look out for a public footpath sign and walk along a road, passing under a railway bridge.

At the next public footpath sign, turn left onto a tarmac path, follow the path to the right and this enclosed path passes under another railway bridge where it joins the banks of the River Anker. ❷ Walk across a field, making for the left hand one of two isolated trees, and then veer slightly right across the rest of the field. Cross a ditch on the far side, continue across the next field to a redundant brick arch, pass under it and keep

Tamworth Town Hall; in front is a statue of Sir Robert Peel

Tamworth Castle stands above the confluence of the rivers Tame and Anker

in the same direction parallel to the river, making for the right field edge.

Continue along it and where the hedge on the right ends, keep ahead across rough open ground and cross a plank footbridge over a ditch. Walk along the right edge of the next field, climb a stile, keep ahead first along an enclosed path and then continue along the left field edge to climb a stile. Here the path forks; take the right hand path, bearing slightly right across the field, and look out for a waymarked post in the hedge in front. Go through a gap in the hedge, keep in the same direction across the next field – now close to the river again – climb a stile and continue towards farm buildings. Climb a stile, keep ahead, passing to the right of the farm, and climb another stile by a bridge over the river.

Continue along a concrete track and at a fork by a public footpath sign, take the left hand track. Where this concrete track turns left, keep ahead along the right edge of a field and where the hedge on the right ends, keep ahead and climb a stile on the far side of the field. To the right are views over some of the pools of Alvecote Nature Reserve. Walk along the left edge of a field, go through a wide gap, continue along the left edge of the next field, later by woodland on the right, and climb a stile. Immediately turn left over another stile and turn right along the right edge of a field above a pool. After climbing the next stile, keep ahead along a track and

River Anker near Tamworth

where it bends right, turn left over a stile, turn right and veer slightly right across the next field towards the hilltop village of Shuttington.

Go through a gate, walk across a field, climb a stile and follow a faint path gently uphill across the next field to a stile. Climb it, head through a narrow belt of trees to climb another stile and continue to a road in the village. ❸ The mainly Georgian church is a short distance ahead but the route continues to the right, heading downhill. Turn right again at a T-junction, follow the road around a left bend, cross a bridge over the River Anker and take the first road on the left (Alvecote Lane). Walk through the small village of Alvecote, follow the

The meagre remains of Alvecote Priory

road around a left bend to keep parallel to the railway line and turn right to cross a bridge over the railway. Immediately cross a canal bridge and keep ahead for 91 m (100 yards) to Alvecote Priory and picnic site. ❹

ℹ️ Alvecote was a small Benedictine priory founded in 1159 and dissolved by Henry VIII in 1536. The meagre remains date from the fourteenth century.

The surrounding pools that make up a nature reserve managed by the Warwickshire Wildlife Trust are the result of mining subsidence and subsequent flooding. These pools and the woodland around them illustrate how an attractive landscape can be created from a previously industrial eyesore.

🚶 Return to the canal bridge, cross it, turn right to the towpath and turn sharp right to pass under the bridge. Continue along the towpath, passing Alvecote Marina, for nearly 3.2 km (2 miles) as far as Bridge 71.

ℹ️ Construction of the Coventry Canal began in 1768 and it was opened in 1790. It runs from the Trent and Mersey Canal at Fradley Junction to Coventry, where it links up with the Oxford Canal.

🚶 In front of the bridge, turn right along a path to a road ❺ and keep along it for 800 m (0.5 miles) to a railway viaduct. In front of the viaduct bear right onto a tarmac footpath and cycle track and continue beside the River Anker again, passing under the viaduct and two road bridges. To the right there are several footbridges over the river that take you onto paths that lead up to the castle and any of them will do. Keep to the right of the castle and cross a footbridge over the foundations of the medieval gatehouse to emerge onto Market Street in front of the town hall.

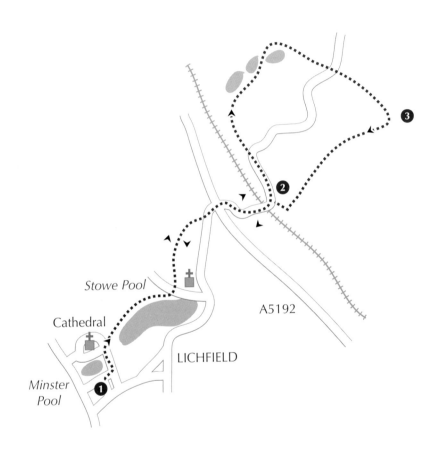

Stowe Pool

Cathedral

Minster
Pool

LICHFIELD

A5192

1

2

3

WALK 10

Around Lichfield

LENGTH:	7.2 km (4.5 miles)
TIME:	2 hours
TERRAIN:	Flat walking along tarmac paths at the beginning and end and field paths in between
START/PARKING:	Lichfield, Market Square, GR SK117096. Pay car parks in the centre of Lichfield
BUS/TRAIN:	Buses and trains from Birmingham, Tamworth, Stafford and all the surrounding towns
REFRESHMENTS:	Pubs and cafes at Lichfield
MAP:	O.S. Explorer 232 – Nuneaton & Tamworth and O.S. Explorer 245 – The National Forest

From the centre of Lichfield, the walk takes you by Stowe Pool for a short circuit of the pleasant and gentle countryside of the Trent valley to the north of the city. On the final stretch there are fine views of the three spires of Lichfield Cathedral. Make sure that you leave plenty of time to explore this attractive historic city.

❶ Apart from its cathedral, Lichfield's main claim to fame is that it was the birthplace of Dr Johnson, the renowned eighteenth-century literary figure and compiler of the first English dictionary. The house in which he was born in

The west front of Lichfield Cathedral

1709 is in one corner of the Market Square. Tel: 01543 264972

Also in the square is the large nineteenth-century St Mary's church, now housing the Lichfield Heritage Centre. Tel: 01543 256611

❶ With your back to St Mary's church, walk along Dam Street towards the cathedral. Just after passing the end of Minster Pool, the route turns right along Reeve Lane but keep ahead into the close in order to visit the cathedral.

With its ornate west front and three spires rising above the surrounding pools, Lichfield is one of the most beautiful of English cathedrals and has the distinction of being the only triple-spired medieval cathedral in the country. It is also one of the earliest in England, founded by St Chad in 669.

The present church was built between the late twelfth and early fourteenth centuries and, despite a chequered history and much restoration, it is a superb example of Gothic architecture. The damage mostly occurred during the Civil War when the cathedral close was repeatedly bombarded by both Royalists and Parliamentarians. The interior was used as a barracks and stables and the central tower was destroyed. The tower was subsequently rebuilt and the cathedral restored during the late seventeenth century. More extensive restoration took place during the nineteenth century.

Apart from the three spires and the ornate west front, one of the chief glories of Lichfield Cathedral is the sixteenth-century stained glass in the Lady Chapel, brought here from a Belgian monastery. The cathedral is further enhanced by its setting, in a secluded close on the north side of the old city lined by dignified seventeenth- and eighteenth-century buildings. Tel: 01543 306100

🚶 After turning right along Reeve Lane, continue along a tarmac path beside Stowe Pool. At the end of the pool where the path curves right towards St Chad's church, turn left down steps off the embankment and cross a road.

ℹ️ St Chad's church lies at the northern end of Stowe Pool, only 800 m (0.5 miles) from the cathedral. The original church was Saxon, founded in the seventh century by St Chad, first bishop of Lichfield, but the present church is medieval and dates mainly from the thirteenth century. Like the cathedral it was badly damaged during the Civil War when it was used as a military storehouse and had to be extensively restored afterwards. It was during this restoration that the upper part of the nave was rebuilt in brick. Further restoration was carried out in the Victorian era.

🚶 Continue along the enclosed footpath and cycle track opposite to emerge onto a road. Turn left towards a T-junction, turn right beside the main road – still on the signed footpath and cycle track – turn left to cross the road, turn right and then turn left into Netherstowe Lane. Immediately after crossing a railway bridge, ❷ turn left along a lane and where it bends right, keep ahead along a narrow enclosed path.

After climbing a stile, the path curves right across a field, curves slightly left and then right again and continues along the left field edge. Several pools can be seen over to the left. Where the edge veers slightly right, look out for a yellow waymark on a tree, turn left through a belt of trees and continue along a clear path beside a pool on the right. Follow the path around a right bend and where it bends left, keep ahead across a causeway between two pools, bear left through a young plantation and cross another causeway to a kissing gate.

The three spires of Lichfield Cathedral

St Chad's church from across Stowe Pool

Go through, walk across a field to the far right hand corner and go through a gate onto a lane. Turn left and immediately turn right through a gate into a field. Head across it, making for the far left hand corner but before reaching it, look out for a stile in the fence on the left. Climb it, turn right along a fence-lined path, climb another stile and walk diagonally across the next field to a stile in the corner.

Climb it, continue along a right field edge and in the corner, turn right over a stile ❸ and walk along the left edge of the next field. At a hedge gap, bear first left and then right to continue along the right edge of the next field. After about 183 m (200 yards) – and by a large tree – bear left and head across the field to a gate in the corner. Go through, walk across a field, go through another gate and head across the next field to a stile.

After climbing it, maintain the same direction across the next field and on the far side, turn right along the left edge and climb a stile onto a lane. Turn left over a railway bridge, ❷ here picking up the outward route and retrace your steps to the start.

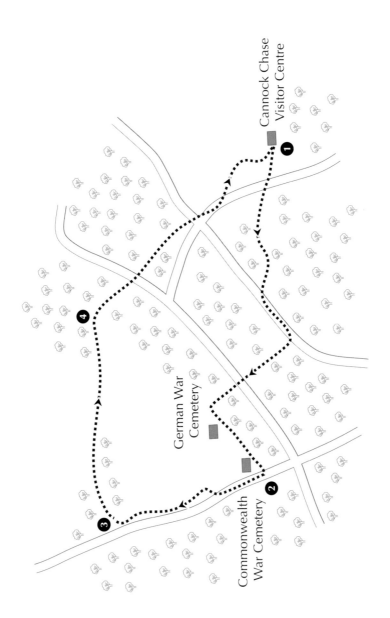

Cannock Chase
Visitor Centre

German War
Cemetery

Commonwealth
War Cemetery

WALK 11

Cannock Chase

LENGTH:	8 km (5 miles)
TIME:	2.5 hours
TERRAIN:	Clear paths across forest and heath
START/PARKING:	Cannock Chase Visitor Centre, signposted from A513 at Rugeley and A460 at Hednesford, GR SJ004154
BUS/TRAIN:	The Chase Hopper bus service, which operates throughout spring, summer and autumn on Sundays and Bank Holiday Mondays, links Cannock, Rugeley and Hednesford with the Visitor Centre and other places in Cannock Chase. For information phone 01543 462261
REFRESHMENTS:	Café at the Visitor Centre, café near the Katyn Memorial
MAP:	O.S. Explorer 244 – Cannock Chase & Chasewater

Cannock Chase is the largest area of lowland heath surviving in the Midlands and the combination of forest and heath, plus extensive views and good clear paths and tracks, makes it a popular destination for local walkers. As well as its scenic and recreational qualities, the chase has a strong military heritage and throughout the route there are a number of reminders of this.

ℹ In the Middle Ages the vast royal hunting ground of Cannock Forest extended over much of south Staffordshire between Stafford, Lichfield and Walsall. A chase was a private hunting area, as opposed to a royal one, and in 1290 Edward I granted part of the forest to the bishop of Lichfield as his private chase. In the sixteenth century the chase passed to the Paget family (later Marquises of Anglesey) who began the exploitation of the chase's coal and iron reserves. Coal mines were sunk on the southern part of the chase, between the seventeenth and nineteenth centuries many of the trees were felled to feed the iron industries of the nearby Black Country and much of the area reverted to open heathland. This was ideal terrain for troop training and during the world wars of the twentieth century, army training camps were set up plus a military

Typical landscape of Cannock Chase

Commonwealth War Cemetery in Cannock Chase

hospital and a German prisoner of war camp.

From the 1920s onwards much of the chase was taken over by the Forestry Commission and large plantations of mainly Scots and Corsican pine were established. Therefore nowadays Cannock Chase is mainly a mixture of conifer forest and heathland but sizeable remnants of ancient woodland still survive.

Historically this walk emphasises the military role of the chase. The area of Brindley Heath around the Visitor Centre was the site of a large military hospital during World War I. but the buildings were demolished in the 1950s. There was also the nearby RAF Camp at Hednesford, built in the late 1930s and closed in 1956. The Visitor Centre occupies the site of the officers' mess. Tel: 01543 871773

(🚶) ❶ With your back to the entrance to the Visitor Centre, take the blue- and red- waymarked path across a picnic area, cross a drive and keep ahead to a road. Cross over, continue through a small parking and picnic area and bear left along a track. At a fork just ahead, take the right hand track (still on the blue-and red-waymarked trail) and head gently downhill, curving right to a T-junction.

Turn left into a dip and at a crossways, turn right onto a track which emerges onto a road at Brindley Bottom car park. Cross over, take the uphill path ahead to emerge onto another road, turn left and at a public bridleway sign, turn right beside a barrier onto a track The track descends to a T-junction. Turn left, passing the German War Cemetery, and keep ahead along a tarmac drive to a road by the Commonwealth War Cemetery. ❷

❶ The German War Cemetery was created in the 1960s and around 5000 war dead – soldiers, sailors, airmen, prisoners of war – from both world wars were brought here to be re-interred. The Commonwealth War Cemetery mainly contains the graves of British and New Zealand servicemen.

(🚶) Turn right and after 400 m (0.25 miles), turn right, at a public bridleway sign, along a track to a parking area. Turn left beside a vehicle barrier and immediately turn left again onto a path which initially heads back towards the road and then curves right to continue across the open heathland parallel to the road. After curving right to a crossways, turn left along a path through trees to a tarmac track and turn right. ❸ Here you join the Heart of England Way for the remainder of the walk.

❶ Over to the left is the Katyn Memorial, erected in memory of the thousands of Polish soldiers killed by the Soviet authorities in Katyn Forest in 1940.

Ⓚ Keeping ahead at all junctions, follow the track through woodland and across heathland into the lovely Sherbrook valley. After climbing gently out of the valley along a broad track, turn right ❹ along a track which ascends to a road. Cross over, walk along the path ahead to a T-junction, turn right and take the first path on the left. Repeat the process at the next T-junction and the path emerges onto a road at a junction.

Keep ahead in the Hednesford direction along Marquis Drive and where the road curves right, bear left along a tarmac drive (still Marquis Drive). Take the first turning on the right and turn left to return to the Visitor Centre.

Woodland and Heath in Cannock Chase

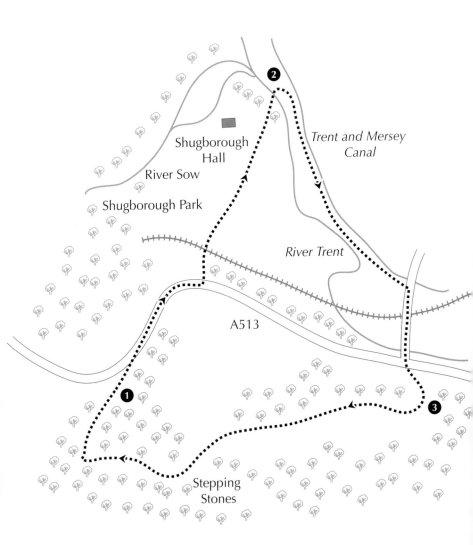

WALK 12

Trent Valley and the Northern Fringes of Cannock Chase

LENGTH:	8.9 km (5.5 miles)
TIME:	2.5 hours
TERRAIN:	Parkland, canal towpath and forest tracks
START/PARKING:	The Punchbowl car park, off the A513, 1.2 km (0.75 miles) east of Milford, GR SJ984208. If busy, there is another car park (Satnall Hills) on the other side of the road.
BUS/TRAIN:	Buses from Lichfield and Stafford
REFRESHMENTS:	Café at Shugborough Hall
MAP:	O.S. Explorer 244 – Cannock Chase & Chasewater

The walk falls into three clearly defined sections. First there is an easy stroll across Shugborough Park with fine views of both the house and parkland and over the Trent valley. Next comes an attractive stretch along a canal towpath between the Trent and Mersey Canal and the River Trent. The finale is a beautiful woodland walk, passing by the largest area of ancient oak woodland in Cannock Chase.

❶ Facing the A513, turn right and walk along the road for just over 800 m (0.5 mile). At first there is a verge and later a path on the left side of the road. At a public bridleway sign to Great Haywood, turn left through a gate and walk along a tarmac path through trees to another gate.

Go through and keep ahead along the drive through Shugborough Park. Cross a railway bridge, take the right hand drive at a fork and at the next fork, continue along the left hand drive, passing to the right of Park Farm. The façade of Shugborough Hall can be seen over to the left and where the drive bears left to the hall, go through the gate in front and the route continues along a fence-lined tarmac track.

ⓘ The land around Shugborough on the northern fringes of Cannock Chase originally formed part of the estate of the bishops of Lichfield but in 1624 it was purchased by the Anson family, later earls of Lichfield. In 1693 William Anson began the transformation of the modest manor house into the present grand mansion.

The arch seen over to the left soon after entering the park, the Anson Arch, was erected to commemorate the circumnavigation of the world by Admiral George Anson

Distant view of the façade of Shugborough Hall

in the 1740s and it was largely from the profits of this voyage that his elder brother, Thomas, was able to have the park landscaped and continue with the enlargement of the house shortly afterwards. It was enlarged again towards the end of the eighteenth century when Wyatt added the eight columns that form the grand portico that extends across the whole width of the house, one of its most striking external features.

There is a lot to see and do at Shugborough. A tour of the interior of the house takes you through some of the grand state rooms – dining room, library, drawing room, saloon and bedrooms – plus the servant's quarters. It also includes the Anson Room that contains memorabilia of Admiral George Anson. Outside there are gardens to enjoy, including a walled garden, and grounds to explore where you can take riverside walks beside the Sow and visit the various follies and monuments that are dotted around. In addition there is Park Farm, a working agricultural museum that shows you how an estate farm functioned around 1800.

Tel: 01889 881323

(人) **At the end of the parkland, cross Essex Bridge over the River Trent – just upstream from here the Trent is joined by the River Sow – and in front of the canal bridge, turn right beside a gate onto the towpath of the Trent and Mersey Canal. ❷ Now follows 1.6 km (1 mile) of very attractive walking beside the tree-lined canal, with more fine views across the river and parkland to the right of Shugborough Hall and the wooded slopes of Cannock Chase on the horizon.**

❶ The picturesque 14-arched Essex Bridge over the River Trent was built in 1550 by the Earl of Essex. Its purpose was to make it easier to cross the river while on hunting expeditions in the local woodlands.

The sixteenth-century Essex Bridge over the River Trent

The Trent and Mersey Canal was opened in 1777. It linked the River Trent at Shardlow with the River Mersey at Runcorn, a distance of 149 km (93 miles).

After passing under Bridge 72, turn sharp right up steps to a lane and turn left. Go under a railway bridge and after recrossing the Trent you reach the A513 again. Cross it and follow the winding uphill track ahead, curving right through Seven Springs car park. ❸

Two paths lead off from the car park. Take the right hand one (part of the blue-waymarked Sabrina Trail) and at a crossways turn right. Keep on the main path all the while as you climb gently through beautiful woodland. Later you descend into the Sherbrook valley to reach the

Stepping Stones, an idyllic spot. After crossing the stones, turn right at a crossways, in the Punchbowl direction, and continue through the valley below the wooded slopes of Brocton Coppice on the left.

ⓘ This north western area is one of the most popular and attractive parts of Cannock Chase and here you find the finest remaining areas of broadleaved trees. In particular take time to explore Brocton Coppice, the most extensive surviving area of ancient oak woodland in the chase.

⦿ At a crossways turn right along a path which leads through more delightful woodland back to the car park.

The Stepping Stones, an idyllic spot in Cannock Chase

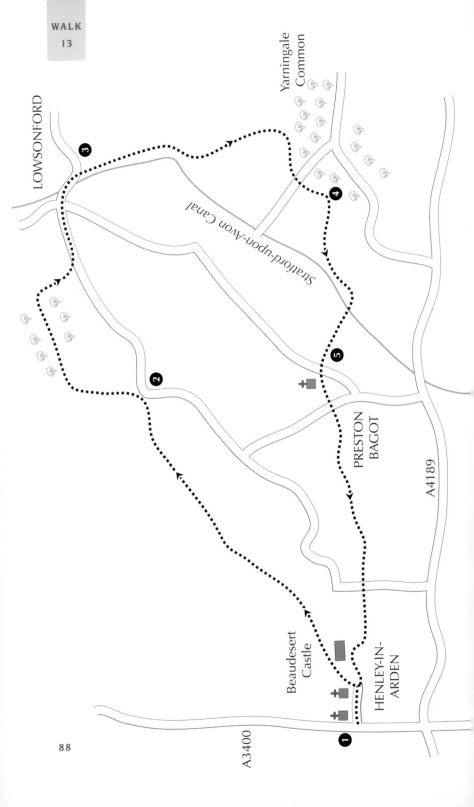

WALK 13

Henley-in-Arden and the Stratford-upon-Avon Canal

LENGTH:	12.1 km (7.5 miles)
TIME:	4 hours
TERRAIN:	Mostly on good, clear paths with a stretch along a canal towpath, several climbs and over 25 stiles to negotiate
START/PARKING:	Henley-in-Arden, by the church in High Street, GR SP151660. Free car parks at Henley
BUS/TRAIN:	Buses and trains from Birmingham and Stratford-upon-Avon
REFRESHMENTS:	Pubs and cafes at Henley, pub at Lowsonford
MAP:	O.S. Explorer 220 – Birmingham

From the centre of Henley-in-Arden you head up over the earthworks of Beaudesert Castle and follow a well-wooded and undulating route to the canalside hamlet of Lowsonford. After a pleasant stretch by the Stratford-upon-Avon Canal the route continues to Yarningale Common and on to the isolated hilltop church at Preston Bagot. From here you return to Henley. The walk has plenty of variety and is quite hilly in places but from the higher points there are splendid views over the rolling, well-wooded Arden countryside.

 Henley-in-Arden's 1.6 km (1 mile) long High Street is lined on both sides by attractive old brick and half-timbered buildings. About half way along are the timber-framed Guild Hall and St John's church, both built in the fifteenth century, the starting point of the walk. Towards the southern end of the street is the Henley Heritage Centre and next door is one of Henley's most popular attractions, the famous ice cream parlour. As its name suggests, Henley lies in the heart of the old Forest of Arden and the numerous inns and other eating places along the High Street are an indication that it was once an important coaching stop on the former main road between Birmingham, Stratford and Oxford.

Henley-in-Arden's lengthy High Street

Looking over Henley-in-Arden form the summit of the vanished Beaudesert Castle; both Beaudesert and Henley church towers can be seen

❶ The first part of the route follows the well-waymarked Heart of England Way. Begin by walking down Beaudesert Lane to Beaudesert church and the castle mound.

The church at Beaudesert is only a few hundred yards from the one at Henley but this is because in the Middle Ages Henley and Beaudesert were separate parishes despite their close proximity. This church is about three centuries older than the one up the road, built in the twelfth century and noted for its fine Norman arches.

It is situated at the foot of the castle of the De Montforts, originally a Norman motte and bailey castle constructed in the eleventh century. It was later rebuilt in stone but the castle declined after the fall of the De Montfort family following the battle of Evesham in 1265. It was later dismantled and all that remains is the massive earthworks, across which the next part of the walk proceeds.

(walker icon) Where the lane ends, go through a kissing gate and bear slightly left onto a path that heads up over the earthworks of the now vanished castle. After descending from the castle mound, the route continues over another hill and at the top keeps along the right edge of a field. At a fork a waymark directs you to take the right hand path to a stile.

Climb it, walk diagonally across a field, climb another stile and turn left along the left inside edge of a narrow belt of trees. At a Heart of England post, turn right to emerge from the trees and keep straight across the next field. On the far side, cross a tarmac track, keep ahead through a belt of trees and continue first along the left field edge and later across the field to a kissing gate.

Go through, walk through another belt of trees and continue across the next field. Go through a kissing gate, keep along the right field edge and then head across the field to go through a hedge gap. Walk along a left field edge, go through another kissing gate, continue along a right field edge and on joining a tarmac track, bear right along it to a lane. ❷ Turn left and immediately after a right bend, turn left along an enclosed tarmac drive. Just after crossing a bridge over a disused railway line, turn right through a gate and walk along the right edge of a field, by woodland on the right. The path later veers left to join a track which curves left to go through a hedge gap.

Turn right and continue by the left edge of trees, bending left at a waymarked post to enter the wood. The path bends right, heads uphill and at the top emerges from the trees to continue along the right edge of a field. Climb a stile in the corner, immediately turn right over another one, walk along an enclosed path – leaving the Heart of England Way which turns left off this path – and pass beside a gate onto a lane.

Turn left and head gently downhill into Lowsonford. At

a T-junction turn left for the Fleur de Lys pub, otherwise turn right over the canal bridge. ❸ Turn right through a gate and turn left to continue along the towpath of the Stratford Canal.

🛈 Construction of the Stratford-upon-Avon Canal began in 1793 and was completed in 1816. It runs for about 40.2 km (25 miles) from King's Norton in the suburbs of Birmingham, where it joins the Worcester and Birmingham Canal, to Stratford where it empties into the River Avon.

🚶 After nearly 1.2 km (0.75 miles)– shortly after a right curve – turn left through a kissing gate and follow a winding path through woodland. After crossing a footbridge over a stream, you emerge from the trees and keep ahead across a field, fording a stream to reach a stile. Climb it, keep ahead across the next field – initially along its left edge and later along the right edge – climb another stile and walk along the right edge of a field. Climb a stile in the corner, walk along the left edge of

The isolated hilltop church at Preston Bagot

the next field and climb a stile to enter the woodland of
Yarningale Common.

Keep ahead to a T-junction and turn right along a path
which keeps parallel to the right inside edge of the trees.
The path later widens into a track which bends first right
and then left to emerge onto a lane. Turn right and at a
public footpath sign, turn left along a faint grassy path
and cross a drive to a stile. Climb it, keep ahead along
an enclosed path, climb another stile, continue along the
right inside edge of woodland and turn right over a stile.
❹
Walk along the right edge of the common, climb a
stile and descend along the right edge of a field. At the
bottom, go through a gap in a line of trees and bear left
across a field to a waymarked post on the far side. Bear
left along the right field edge, climb two stiles in quick
succession, keep along a right field edge, go through
a gate and turn right to cross a footbridge over the
Stratford Canal. Go through a gate, turn right to cross a
bridge, take the winding path ahead through trees and
bushes and cross another bridge over a stream.

Go through a gate and walk across a field, later
keeping by its left edge to go through a hedge gap.
Continue across the next field and go through a kissing
gate onto a lane. ❺ Take the track opposite, go through
a kissing gate and walk along the right field edge, passing
to the left of Preston Bagot church.

❶ From the small hilltop Norman church at Preston Bagot,
the views over the countryside of the Forest of Arden are
superb. It was originally built in the twelfth century and
comprehensively restored in 1879 when the bell turret was
added.

🧍 After going through a kissing gate, head downhill along
an enclosed path and go through another kissing gate

The earthworks of the motte are all that remain of Beaudesert Castle

onto a lane. Cross over, go through a gate and walk along the right edgeof two fields. Keep ahead across the third field to a stile, climb it and continue along the right edge of first a field and then a young plantation. The route now keeps in a fairly straight line along the edge of or across the middle of a succession of fields, finally climbing a stile onto a tree-lined path. Turn right, turn left over a stile and continue along the right edge of more fields, negotiating a series of gates and stiles, before emerging onto a road.

Turn right, turn left over a stile and walk along a right field edge. Where the edge curves left, turn right over a stile, turn left over another one and descend a flight of steps through woodland. Keep ahead across a children's' play area to a gate, go through and walk along an enclosed tarmac track. Cross a road, keep ahead along an enclosed track and after passing beside a barrier, the way continues along an enclosed path which bends right beside a school fence on the left.

In front of a kissing gate, turn left to continue beside the school fence and keep ahead to a road. Pick up another enclosed path which emerges onto a lane by Beaudesert church and follow the lane back to the start.

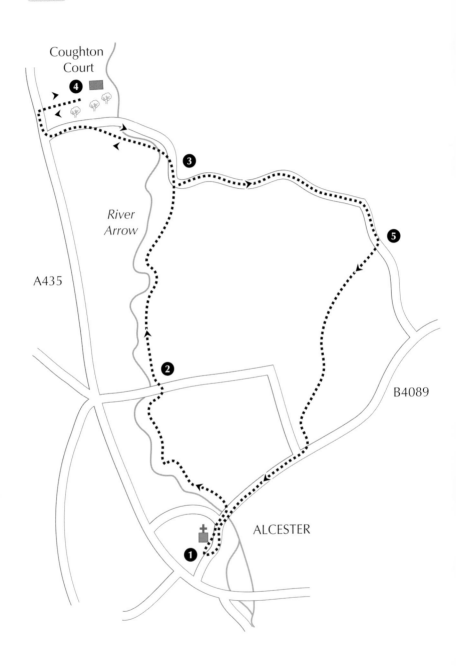

Coughton
Court

4

*River
Arrow*

A435

3

5

2

B4089

1

ALCESTER

WALK 14

Alcester, River Arrow and Coughton Court

LENGTH:	11.3 km (7 miles)
TIME:	3.5 hours
TERRAIN:	Field and riverside paths and one quiet lane, mostly flat country
START/PARKING:	Alcester, top of High Street by the church, GR SP090575. Free car parks at Alcester
BUS/TRAIN:	Buses from Stratford-upon-Avon, Redditch and Evesham
REFRESHMENTS:	Pubs and cafes at Alcester, café at Coughton Court
MAP:	O.S. Explorer 205 – Stratford-upon-Avon & Evesham and O.S. Explorer 220 – Birmingham

The first half of the walk between Alcester and Coughton Court is mainly across fields beside the meandering River Arrow. On the return leg a gentle climb onto a low ridge gives you extensive views over Alcester and the surrounding countryside of the Forest of Arden.

❶ The pleasant old town of Alcester has a number of dignified Georgian houses in the High Street, a seventeenth-century Town Hall near the church and an outstanding collection of picturesque brick and half-

Alcester parish church

timbered cottages in Malt Mill Lane. With its imposing fourteenth-century tower, the church looks like a typical late medieval town church from the outside but has a surprisingly classical interior. This is because most of it was rebuilt in 1729 through a combination of neglect and a fire.

❶ Start by walking along the pedestrianised Butter Street to the left of the church to the Old Town Hall. Continue along Henley Street and after the road bears right, it becomes Kinwarton Road.

Just after crossing a bridge over the River Arrow, turn left onto a path beside the Greig Lifestyles building and continue along a well-surfaced path that follows the twists and turns of the river along the left edge of a sports field to reach a T-junction to the right of a footbridge. Turn right and at a waymarked post, take the first path on the left between trees and bushes which

emerges briefly onto a road before bearing left and then bending right to the B4089. ❷

Cross over and at a public footpath sign, take the path opposite which continues beside the tree-lined River Arrow. At a fork, take the left hand path to keep along the left field edge, go through a hedge gap and continue along the left field edge. After passing a weir, follow the curve of the river round to a gate, pass beside it and continue to a waymarked post where the river curves left. Keep ahead parallel to the left field edge, go through a gate and head diagonally across the next field, making for the far right corner where you go through a kissing gate onto a lane. ❸

Tudor buildings in Alcester

Turn left and at a public footpath sign, turn left again to cross a footbridge over the Arrow and head straight across a field. Go through a kissing gate, keep in the same direction across the next field and go through a kissing gate onto the lane by the Roman Catholic church at Coughton.

In order to visit Coughton Court, turn left along the lane to the main road. Turn right and turn right again through a kissing gate and follow a path across grassland. Cross a track, go through a gate onto a tarmac drive in front of the Anglican church ❹ and turn left to the house.

ⓘ In 1605 Coughton Court was in the forefront of one of the most dramatic episodes in English history, the Gunpowder Plot. It was the home of the Throckmortons, a Roman Catholic family, and some of the relatives of the Catholic conspirators were using the house as a refuge when they heard the news, on the morning of 6 November, that the plot had been discovered.

Coughton is a fine example of a Tudor house and dates from around 1530. The north and south wings were built at right angles to the gatehouse, creating a most attractive courtyard. Inside there are many family portraits and the rooms possess an impressive collection of furniture, tapestries and porcelain. The panelling in the dining room is particularly noteworthy. Visitors can also enjoy the walled gardens and take a riverside stroll in the grounds.

The two nearby churches – one Anglican and the other Catholic – mirror the ups and downs of both the Throckmorton family and the house against the turbulent background of English religious history. The Anglican church, the medieval church serving Coughton, was originally Catholic and contains tombs of the Throckmortons but became Protestant after the Reformation and could no longer be the Throckmorton place of worship. The family had to practise their religion in secret

Coughton Court

during periods of persecution and make do with a chapel in the house but following Catholic Emancipation in 1829 and in an age of greater toleration, a new Roman Catholic church was built in 1853.

🚶 **Retrace your steps to where you first joined the lane ❸ and continue along it for about 2 km (1.25 miles), going around several bends. At a public footpath sign opposite a barn, turn right, ❺ walk across a field and head gently uphill now along the left field edge. Go through a kissing gate, keep ahead over the brow of the hill and look out for where you turn left through a gate and turn right to continue along a right field edge. In the corner keep ahead through a hedge gap, go through a kissing gate into the next field, go through another kissing gate and veer right away from the edge to a trig point. Although standing at the modest height of only 66 m (217 feet), its position on a broad ridge makes it a commanding all round viewpoint.**

Continue past the trig point, heading gently downhill into a belt of trees and follow a winding path downhill through the trees to a road. Turn right and the road leads back to the town centre of Alcester.

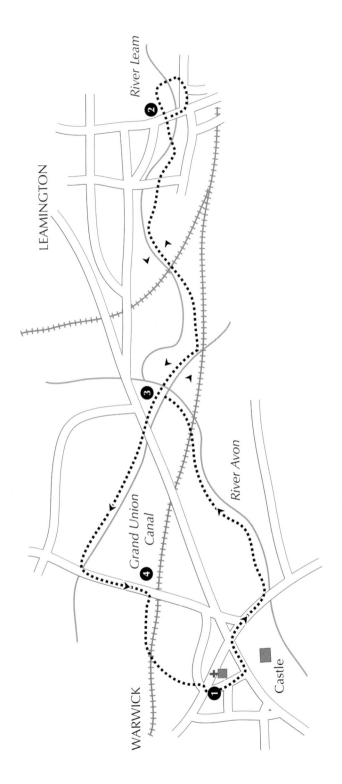

River Leam

LEAMINGTON

River Avon

Grand Union
Canal

WARWICK

Castle

❶ ❷ ❸ ❹

WALK 15

Warwick and Leamington

LENGTH:	11.3 km (7 miles)
TIME:	3.5 hours
TERRAIN:	Mainly riverside paths through a succession of parks, also a canal towpath and some road walking
START/PARKING:	Warwick, St Mary's church, GR SP282650. Plenty of pay car parks in the centre of Warwick
BUS/TRAIN:	Buses from Stratford-upon-Avon, Leamington, Coventry and most surrounding towns; trains from Birmingham, Leamington and Solihull
REFRESHMENTS:	Pubs and cafes at Warwick, pubs and cafes at Leamington
MAP:	O.S. Explorer 221 – Coventry & Warwick

Warwick and Leamington are separate but adjoining towns and when driving between them, it is difficult to work out where one ends and the other begins as there is no break in the built-up area. But beside the three waterways that link them – the rivers Avon and Leam and the Grand Union Canal – a series of almost adjacent parks creates an attractive and peaceful green corridor. The two towns could hardly be more different: the great medieval monuments and half-timbered Tudor buildings of Warwick contrasting with the Regency elegance of the spa town of Leamington.

ℹ️ Much of the grand medieval collegiate church of St Mary was destroyed during the great fire that swept through Warwick in 1694 and it was rebuilt shortly afterwards in the reign of Queen Anne. The lofty tower, 53 m (174 feet) high, is a distinctive landmark for miles around. Fortunately the magnificent fifteenth-century Beauchamp Chapel survived the fire. It contains the tombs of two earls of Warwick but the most prominent tomb is that of Richard Dudley, Earl of Leicester, the favourite of Elizabeth I who lived at nearby Kenilworth Castle.

❶ Facing St Mary's church, turn right down Church Street to a crossroads and keep ahead down Castle Street. Turn left along Castle Lane to a T-junction and just to the left is the much restored East Gate, one of

The classic view of Warwick Castle from the bridge over the River Avon

River Avon at Warwick

the entrances into the medieval town. Turn right and walk down to the bridge over the River Avon, from where there is a particularly memorable view of Warwick Castle.

ⓘ Warwick Castle is one of the grandest in Britain and one of the few to successfully make the transition from a medieval fortress to a later palatial residence. The first castle was built soon after the Norman Conquest on a site of an earlier Saxon fortification. Little remains of this and the present building dates mainly from the fourteenth century. Particularly outstanding are the great gatehouse and the two massive towers, Caesar's Tower and Guy's Tower, which stand at either end of the walls that flank it. Although medieval looking from the outside, much of the interior was reconstructed in the seventeenth and later centuries when successive owners modernised the castle and transformed it into a more comfortable home. In the lavishly decorated state rooms there are fine examples of

Peaceful scene on the Grand Union Canal between Warwick and Leamington

paintings and furniture and the fourteenth-century Great Hall contains an extensive display of arms and armour. As a contrast visitors can also take a look at the dungeon and there are also 60 acres of gardens and grounds to explore.

During its long history, Warwick Castle has passed through many hands but probably the best known of its owners is Richard Neville who was Earl of Warwick in the fifteenth century. He played a pivotal role in the Wars of the Roses during which he acquired the nickname of 'Warwick the King Maker' on account of his habit of changing sides.

Tel: 0870 442 2000

At a Centenary Way sign just before the bridge, turn left down steps into St Nicholas Park and continue along a

tarmac path beside the Avon. After passing a footbridge on the right, keep ahead across a strip of grass between houses and the river and look out for where a path leads off to the right to continue as a tree-shaded riverside path. Pass under a railway bridge, keep ahead through trees to an aqueduct and after passing under it, turn left beside it. Turn left up steps to the Grand Union Canal and turn left again along the towpath. ❷

ℹ️ The Grand Union Canal runs from Little Venice in London to Gas Street Basin in Birmingham and is 220 km (137 miles) long. Throughout its length there are 166 locks. It was formed between 1929 and 1932 by the amalgamation of several different canals.

The early nineteenth-century Pump Rooms at Leamington Spa

🚶 At a sign 'Link to Princes Drive' just before a railway
bridge, turn left along an enclosed path and keep along
it to join the bank of the River Leam, a tributary of the
Avon. After crossing a road and passing under a railway
bridge, you continue along a tarmac drive through
Victoria Park, opened in 1897 to commemorate Queen
Victoria's Diamond Jubilee. Go under a road bridge and
after descending steps, turn left to cross a footbridge over
the Leam into the Pump Rooms Gardens, turn right and
the path bears left alongside the Pump Rooms to a road.
❸

ⓘ Leamington – or to give it its full name of Royal
Leamington Spa – is a largely Regency and Victorian town.
It has a number of attractive parks and gardens and its
wide streets and spacious squares, crescents and terraces
are lined with many elegant nineteenth-century houses.
Until the discovery of mineral springs in the 1780s, it was
little more than a village but after that its growth was rapid
as the springs were developed, baths were built and the
town became a fashionable spa where visitors came to
'take the waters'. Among its most prominent buildings are
the Pump Rooms. They first opened in 1814 with 20 baths
and were extended and remodelled several times in the
Victorian period. After the baths closed, the rooms were
adapted for other uses and now serve as an art gallery,
museum, library, assembly rooms and tourist information
centre.

One of the men who played a leading role in the
growth of Leamington was Doctor Jephson who publicised
the healing properties of the spa waters. The Jephson
Gardens, laid out in 1834 and arguably the most beautiful
of Leamington's many parks, were named after him.

🚶 The next part of the walk will give you a brief taster of
the Jephson Gardens. Cross the road to enter them and

keep ahead along the main path. Turn right between
the Restaurant in the Park and the Aviary Coffee shop,
go down steps, turn right and then left and cross a
suspension footbridge over the Leam. Keep ahead to a
road (Priory Terrace), turn right to a T-junction and turn
right again to recross the river and return to the Pump
Rooms. ❸

Retrace your steps to where you first joined the canal
❷ and continue along the towpath as far as bridge 49.
After passing under it, turn sharp right up to a road and
turn right over the bridge. Continue along the road and
in front of a railway bridge, turn right along an enclosed
tarmac track ❹ at the base of the railway embankment.
Beyond the station you continue along an enclosed path
and at a junction of paths, turn left under a railway
bridge and keep ahead along a tree-lined path to a road.

Keep ahead along the road to a T-junction. Turn right
and almost immediately turn left into North Gate Street
to return to St Mary's church.

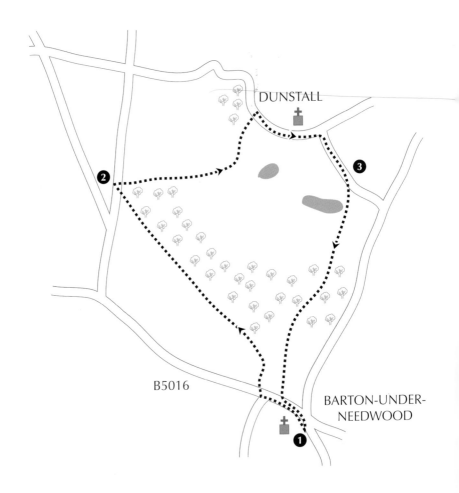

DUNSTALL

2

3

B5016

BARTON-UNDER-
NEEDWOOD

1

WALK 16

The National Forest

LENGTH:	6.4 km (4 miles)
TIME:	2 hours
TERRAIN:	Easy walking along clear paths and tracks across parkland and through woodland
START/PARKING:	Barton-under-Needwood, by the war memorial and church, GR SK188185. Free car park at Barton-under-Needwood
BUS/TRAIN:	Buses from Lichfield and Burton upon Trent
REFRESHMENTS:	Pubs at Barton-under-Needwood
MAP:	O.S. Explorer 245 – The National Forest

This peaceful and relaxing walk serves as an introduction to the National Forest, one of the latest developments in the evolving landscape history of this part of the Midlands area and an exciting long-term project. The route starts in an attractive village, passes through parkland, woodland and an estate hamlet and provides extensive views across the Trent valley.

1 Barton-under-Needwood is situated in the Trent valley below the wooded slopes of the former royal forest of Needwood. It is a pleasant village with a number of attractive old houses and inns. The church, a rare example of a Tudor church, dates from the sixteenth century and occupies the site of an earlier chapel.

⊛ ❶ Facing the Shoulder of Mutton, turn left through the village and at a public bridleway sign, turn right along a track to a gate. Go through, walk along an enclosed track, follow it as it curves left and where the track ends, climb a stile and continue along the left edge of a field.

After climbing a stile, keep ahead along an enclosed track and just after a right bend, look out for where you turn left over a waymarked stile. Turn right along the right field edge and in the corner turn left to continue along the edge. Keep along the right edge of a series of fields and over a succession of stiles, finally climbing a stile onto a lane. ❷ Turn right and almost immediately turn right again through a gate, at a public footpath sign to Dunstall, and keep ahead along a track through trees.

Go through a gate and continue along the track which later descends between trees to another gate. Ahead are superb views over the Trent valley and the lush grassland and pools of the Dunstall Estate, with the spire of Dunstall church prominent. Keep ahead, follow the track around a left bend, go through a gate and turn right by the outbuildings of the Old Hall Farm. Continue to a lane and turn right, passing Dunstall church, and at a junction just beyond it, turn right. To the left is a fine view of Dunstall Hall.

❶ Comprising little more than the hall, a few farms and cottages and the Victorian church, Dunstall is an excellent example of a small estate village. Despite being quite close to a busy main road, the village has a genuine air of tranquillity and remoteness. The hall was constructed in the eighteenth century to replace an earlier one on the site of Old Hall Farm and the church was built in 1853.

⊛ Where the lane bears slightly left, turn right over a stile, ❸ at a public bridleway sign, and head gently downhill along an enclosed path into a dip. The path ascends

equally gently to a gate. Go through, walk through a belt of trees and continue along the right edge of a young plantation. To the left are new trees and to the right mature woodland.

 The young plantations passed on this route are part of the new National Forest, an exciting and imaginative project. The scheme began in the early 1990s and plans to plant millions of new trees in an area that had become seriously depleted of its former woodland cover by the encroachments of agriculture and industry and the growth of towns. Landowners in the area can tender for a grant to help finance the planting of new woods in return for providing public access to them. Eventually it is hoped

The church at Barton-under-Needwood

to create a patchwork of adjoining woodlands that will provide recreational amenities, reclaim land previously scarred by industry and mining and create a physical link between the former medieval forests of Needwood and Charnwood, on the western and eastern fringes of the National Forest respectively.

This new forest extends over an area of about 200 square miles of east Staffordshire, south Derbyshire and west Leicestershire. Although there is still a long way to go, much has already been accomplished in little more than a decade. Over 7 million trees have been planted and the woodland cover increased from 6% to around 17%.

Woodland near Dunstall

Dunstall's nineteenth-century church

⊛ Keep ahead along a tree-lined path, go through a gate and head straight across a field to a fingerpost. Bear slightly left, in the Barton direction, and continue across the field, passing to the right of a pond, to a gate.

Go through, keep ahead by a fence on the right, climb a stile and walk along a hedge-lined track to a gate. Go through and continue along a track which becomes a tarmac drive. On reaching a road, turn left through Barton to return to the start.

New plantations between Barton-under-Needwood and Dunstall,
part of the growing National Forest

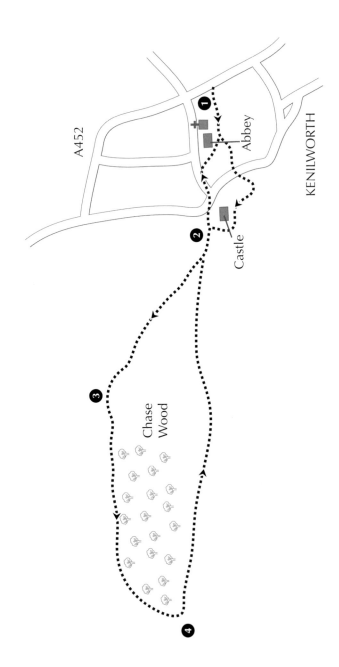

A452

KENILWORTH

Abbey

Castle

Chase
Wood

WALK 17

Around Kenilworth

LENGTH:	8.9 km (5.5 miles)
TIME:	2.5 hours
TERRAIN:	Flat walking across parkland and fields
START/PARKING:	Kenilworth, Abbey Fields, GR SP286725
BUS/TRAIN:	Buses from Coventry, Leamington and Warwick
REFRESHMENTS:	Pubs and cafes at Kenilworth, café at Kenilworth Castle
MAP:	O.S. Explorer 221 – Coventry & Warwick

Many of the wide vistas across the pleasant Warwickshire countryside on this walk are dominated by the imposing red sandstone ruins of Kenilworth Castle, one of the finest in the country. The opening and closing stretches across Abbey Fields, now a park, are both attractive and interesting, with views of the medieval church and scanty remains of an abbey.

❶ From the car park entrance, take the straight, tree-lined tarmac path across the park. Keep to the right of the swimming pool, turn left around the back of the building and turn right to continue along a path between the pool on the right and a stream on the left. Pass beside a barrier to emerge onto a road and turn left to cross the stream.

Kenilworth Castle

Take the first turning on the right into the Castle car park and the entrance to the castle is across the bridge on the right.

ℹ Visiting Kenilworth Castle is like taking a tour through English history and the ruins are among the most complete and impressive in the country. The castle was founded in the early twelfth century by Geoffrey de Clinton but throughout its long and turbulent history it has seen many owners and has frequently alternated between private and royal ownership.

Some of its owners have been among the most powerful men of their day. One was Simon de Montfort, granted the castle by Henry III. He later led a baronial revolt

against the king but was defeated and killed at the battle
of Evesham in 1265. In the following year Kenilworth was
besieged by the king and after nearly 6 months the garrison
surrendered to him, not because of military defeat but
through starvation and disease. The castle subsequently
passed to the Crown and later to the dukes of Lancaster.
One of these was John of Gaunt who began the process
of turning the draughty medieval fortress into a more
comfortable residence by constructing the banqueting hall.
This was continued by Robert Dudley, Earl of Leicester,
the favourite of Elizabeth I. The queen gave him the
castle in 1563 and he began the building of a new suite,
the Leicester Buildings, but was almost bankrupted after
entertaining the queen here on an exceptionally lavish scale
for 19 days in 1575.

The edge of Chase Wood

Kenilworth was one of the most formidable castles
in the country and was surrounded by extensive water
defences. These were needed because it was built on low
lying land with no natural defences. The lakes were drained
after the Civil War and at the same time the castle was
partially demolished. The main surviving buildings fall into
four main periods. First is the formidable Norman keep,
built in the twelfth century. In the late twelfth and early
thirteenth centuries successive monarchs – Henry II, John
and Henry III – strengthened the castle by adding the outer

Cottages on Castle Green at Kenilworth

Little remains of Kenilworth's medieval abbey apart from the barn

walls and towers. John of Gaunt's magnificent fourteenth-century banqueting hall still stands almost complete but for roof and windows and Robert Dudley's Tudor gatehouse and barn survive from his sixteenth-century rebuilding. Tel: 01926 852 078

To continue the walk, keep ahead to a kissing gate, do not go through but turn sharp right along an enclosed track which narrows to a path. Go through a kissing gate, continue below the castle walls and climb a stile onto a track. ❷ Turn left and at a public footpath sign to Chase Lane, turn right through a kissing gate and head diagonally across a field.

On the far side turn right through a hedge gap into the next field and at a fork, take the left hand path to continue diagonally across it. Go through another kissing gate, keep in the same direction across the next field and

The barn stands in lovely woodland

pass through a belt of trees to a kissing gate. After going through it, walk along the right field edge, go through another kissing gate, continue diagonally across the next field and on the far side, go through a kissing gate and turn left onto an enclosed track in front of a house. ❸

The track later continues along the right edge of Chase Wood. At the corner of the wood turn left, head gently downhill and at a waymarked post by a crossways, turn left by the left field edge. ❹ Keep along the left edge of the next three fields and after going through a kissing gate, the way continues along the right edge of the next field to a kissing gate. After going through it, bear left across the next field. This is called The Pleasance and bumps in the ground mark the site of a fifteenth-century royal pleasure palace.

Go through a kissing gate on the far side, walk along an enclosed path and on joining a track, continue along it. Ahead are magnificent views of the castle. You briefly rejoin the outward route but keep along the track to a road. Walk past the attractive cottages lining Castle Green and at a road junction, bear left up Castle Hill. At a yellow waymark on the brow of the hill, turn right through a fence gap to re-enter Abbey Fields and head downhill along a tarmac path towards the pool. Turn right by the remains of the abbey gatehouse and pass to the right of the abbey barn.

❶ Nothing is left of Kenilworth Abbey apart from the vaulted gatehouse and barn. It was founded as a priory by Geoffrey de Clinton, builder of the castle, around 1120 and in the fifteenth century was elevated to the status of an abbey. The nearby medieval church is noted for its fine fourteenth-century tower and spire.

⊛ In front of the swimming pool turn left, here picking up the outward route, and retrace your steps to the start.

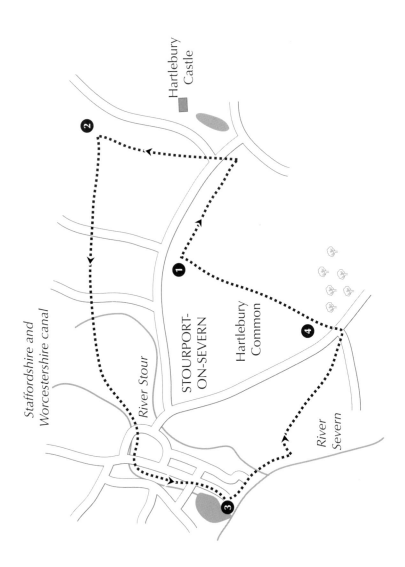

Hartlebury
Castle

STOURPORT-
ON-SEVERN

Hartlebury
Common

*Staffordshire and
Worcestershire canal*

River Stour

*River
Severn*

WALK 18

Hartlebury Common and Stourport-on-Severn

LENGTH:	8 km (5 miles)
TIME:	2.5 hours
TERRAIN:	Field, heathland and riverside paths, disused railway track and canal towpath
START/PARKING:	Hartlebury Common, Leapgate Country Park, Wilden Top car park, off the B4193 between Hartlebury and Stourport-on-Severn, GR SO826715
BUS/TRAIN:	Buses from Kidderminster, Bewdley and Worcester pass through Stourport from where the walk could be picked up at point 3
REFRESHMENTS:	Pubs and cafes at Stourport-on-Severn and several canalside pubs
MAP:	O.S. Explorer 218 – Wyre Forest & Kidderminster

The first and last parts of the route are across the open, breezy, heathery expanses of Hartlebury Common, from where there are fine views over the Severn valley. In between, as a complete contrast, you walk along a disused railway track, beside the Staffordshire and Worcestershire Canal and briefly by the River Severn. The main focal point of the walk is the eighteenth-century canal town of Stourport-on-Severn.

ⓘ Leapgate Country Park mainly comprises the 200 acres of Hartlebury Common but also includes a small area of woodland and the track of the disused Leapgate Old Railway. Hartlebury Common is a surviving area of open, sandy heathland, rare in this part of Worcestershire, and because of this is an important nature reserve. Although the trig point near the start is only 56 m (184 feet) high, it offers fine and extensive all round views over the Severn valley and surrounding countryside. In late summer and early autumn when the heather is out, much of the common is a riot of mauve and purple.

The track of the Leapgate Old Railway is used later on the walk. The railway linked the Kidderminster–Worcester

Canal basin at Stockport-on-Severn

The open heathland of Hartlebury Common

line near Hartlebury with the Severn Valley Railway near Bewdley. Now part of it has been converted into a pleasant and easy walking route.

❶ **With your back to the road, take the path ahead, to the left of an information board, and at a crossways, turn left, passing the trig point. Go through a hedge gap and head gently downhill along an enclosed path to a tarmac drive. Bear right off the drive, cross a track by a gate and go through a hedge gap to continue along the right edge of a field, descending into a dip. Head up an embankment, via steps, to enter a field, turn first right and then left to walk along its right edge and continue along an enclosed path to a gate.**

Go through, keep ahead through trees to a T-junction and turn left, passing farm buildings, to a road. Turn left, take the first lane on the right (Charlton Lane) but immediately bear left onto a straight, hedge-lined track. As the route continues across fields, Hartlebury Castle can be seen over to the right.

ⓘ Since the Middle Ages, Hartlebury Castle has been the palace of the bishops of Worcester. Parts of it date back to the fourteenth century but it was mostly rebuilt in the seventeenth and eighteenth centuries following destruction by fire during the Civil War. The castle is well worth a visit. Some of the bishop's state rooms, including the Great Hall, are open to the public and part of the castle now houses the Worcestershire County Museum. There are picnic areas, visitor centre, gift shop and a café. Tel: 01299 250416

Nearing the end of a field, keep ahead along a path through trees. Soon after crossing a disused railway bridge, turn sharp left ❷ to head down to the track of the former Leapgate Old Railway and turn right along it. Follow the track for about 1.6 km (1 mile) – through deep cuttings, across embankments and over bridges – until you reach a fork. Take the right hand lower path to the canal, turn left to pass under a bridge and follow the canal towpath into Stourport. At York Street Lock the towpath emerges onto a road. Keep ahead down Mart Lane, passing to the left of the canal basins, to the River Severn. ❸

ⓘ Stourport-on-Severn is a creation of the canal age, one of the few towns in England that owes its existence wholly to the building of a canal. James Brindley began the construction of the Staffordshire and Worcestershire Canal in 1766 to link the River Severn with the Trent and

Mersey Canal at Great Haywood. After its opening in 1771, Stourport developed rapidly and a number of industries grew up around the town. Its trade began to decline when a rival and more direct link between the industrial Midlands and the Severn – the Worcester and Birmingham Canal – was opened in 1815 and this accelerated with the coming of the railways.

Some handsome Georgian buildings survive in Stourport town centre and especially around the complex of locks and canal basins between York Street and the River Severn. Nowadays the canal is used mainly by pleasure boats.

Ⓧ **Turn left onto a tarmac riverside path, cross a footbridge at the confluence of the Severn and Stour and in the corner of a field in front of a white house, turn left along an enclosed tarmac path to a road. Turn right, take the first road on the left which bends to the right and immediately turn left onto a track.**

At a footpath post continue along a path to the left of the track, here re-entering Hartlebury Common, and at a fork, take the right hand sandy path which keeps close to the right edge of the common. On emerging onto a road, turn left to a T-junction, turn right and after a few yards, look out for a public footpath sign ❹ where you turn left onto a path through trees. After passing by a row of posts, turn sharp right onto a path which heads uphill through woodland, take the first path on the left and as you continue up, there are fine views to the left over the heathery expanses of the common to Stourport and the Severn valley.

At a waymarked post at the top, bear right – here joining a Heather Trail – across an area of heathland dotted with trees. Later you join a Horse Trail and follow the regular Horse Trail purple-waymaked posts along a fairly straight sandy path which leads back to the start.

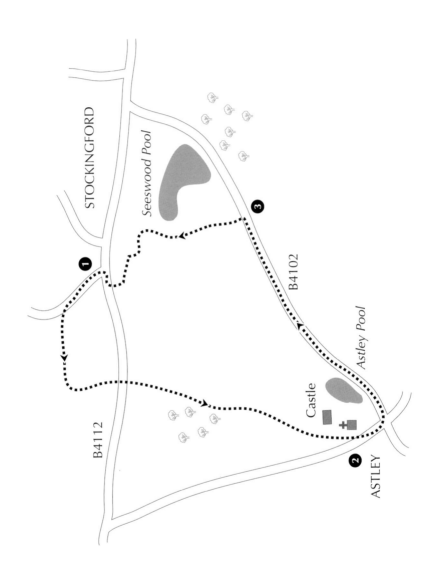

STOCKINGFORD

Seeswood Pool

B4102

Astley Pool

B4112

Castle

ASTLEY

WALK 19

George Eliot Country

LENGTH:	6.4 km (4 miles)
TIME:	2 hours
TERRAIN:	Mostly well-signed field paths and one stretch along a road; 14 kissing gates
START/PARKING:	Stockingford, Park Lane, off the B4112 on the western edge of Nuneaton, GR SP321912. Park carefully on Park Lane near the primary school or in one of the adjacent roads
BUS/TRAIN:	Buses from Nuneaton
REFRESHMENTS:	None
MAP:	O.S. Explorer 232 – Nuneaton & Tamworth

The Victorian novelist George Eliot was born and brought up in the pleasant and open Warwickshire countryside close to the mines and industries of the Nuneaton area. This easy walk gives you the flavour of the terrain which inspired some of her work and visits a hamlet with a church and ruined castle closely associated with her life.

❶ George Eliot, one of the foremost English novelists of the Victorian era, was born in 1819 at South Farm on the Arbury estate near Nuneaton and died at London in 1880. Her real name was Mary Anne Evans and according to her, she used a male pen name in order to be taken more

Astley Park

seriously as a novelist as female writers were often thought of at the time as purely writers of romantic fiction. Her best known works include Adam Bede, The Mill on the Floss, Middlemarch and Silas Marner. She used places and the countryside around her home town of Nuneation as the setting for many of her works. Later she moved to Coventry and then to London. She achieved a certain amount of notoriety in the prim world of Victorian England by living for many years with a married man, George Henry Lewes.

For details on visiting Arbury Hall, phone 024 7638 2804

(人) **❶ Begin by walking along Park Lane away from the main road, with the school on your left. At a public footpath sign, turn left through a kissing gate and take the path ahead, by a wire fence on the right, to another kissing gate. Go through, head down into a dip along a left field edge and about 46 m (50 yards) before reaching the field corner, turn left through a wide hedge gap and head gently uphill along the left field edge.**

Go through a kissing gate onto the B4112, cross over, go through the kissing gate opposite and walk across a field, descending to cross a brook. Pass through a line of trees, keep ahead across a field towards the left edge of woodland and go through a kissing gate in the far left corner. Turn right along the right edge of the next field by woodland on the right, go through a kissing gate and keep ahead to go through another one. Continue across a field, making for its left edge and keep along it to the corner where you turn left through a kissing gate and cross a plank footbridge.

Turn right along a track and just after passing a farmhouse where the track curves left, keep ahead into a field and continue straight across it, in the direction of Astley church tower. On the far side go through a hedge gap to the left of a tree, cross a plank footbridge and head across the next field. Go through another hedge gap – this time to the right of a tree – cross another plank footbridge, walk across the field and on the far side go through one more hedge gap and turn left along an enclosed path. From this path there is a fine view of the church and castle ruins at Astley. After going through a

The forlorn remains of Astley Castle

gate onto a tarmac track, a left turn into the churchyard allows you to visit the church and take a closer look at the remains of the castle.

❶ The delightful hamlet of Astley, together with its castle and church, is used as a location in George Eliot's novel 'Scenes of Clerical Life' in which it is called Knebley. Astley Castle was originally a twelfth-century manor house but in 1266 it was converted into a castle when the owner was given permission to crenellate i.e. provide it with battlements. It was extended in the fifteenth century and later by the Grey family. One well-known member of that family, Lady Jane Grey, spent some of her childhood here. This unfortunate girl was installed as queen for just nine days in 1553 in an unsuccessful attempt to prevent the accession of the Catholic Queen Mary I, an event that led to her subsequent execution. The castle later became a hotel but was destroyed by a fire in 1978 and is now a romantic-looking ruin.

The church was where George Eliot's parents were married in 1813. It is an impressive building with an imposing west tower but was at one time even more impressive as the nave of the present church is only the chancel of what was originally a much larger collegiate church built in 1343. This church fell into ruin and partly collapsed in the sixteenth century. Inside are effigies of the Greys.

🚶 **Keep ahead along the tarmac track to a road. ❷ Turn left and at a crossroads turn left again. Now comes just over 1.6 km (1 mile) of road walking but the road is fairly quiet, there is a footpath all the way and there are pleasant views across parkland both sides – Astley on the left and Arbury, birthplace of George Eliot, to the right. There is a particularly memorable view near the start of Astley church looking across Astley Pool.**

At public footpath and Centenary Way signs, turn left
through a hedge gap ❸ and walk along the left edge
of a field to a kissing gate. Go through, cross a plank
footbridge, go up steps and continue across a field to
another kissing gate. After going through it, keep in the
same direction across the next field, heading down to
a kissing gate. Go through, keep ahead past the end of
Seeswood Pool on the right, go through another kissing
gate and head gently uphill across a field to a waymarked
post.

Turn left to walk along the right field edge, go through
a kissing gate in the corner and bear slightly right across
the next field to a kissing gate on the far side. Go
through and walk along an enclosed path to the B4112.
Turn right and the first road on the left brings you back
to the starting point.

The church at Astley was where George Eliot's parents were married

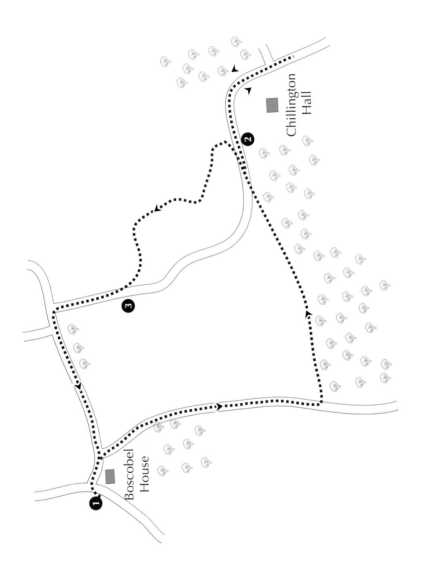

Chillington Hall

Boscobel House

WALK 20

Boscobel House and Chillington Hall

LENGTH:	9.7 km (6 miles)
TIME:	3 hours
TERRAIN:	Field and woodland paths, quiet lanes and one stretch of road walking at the start
START/PARKING:	Boscobel House, on minor road about 2 km (1.25 miles) south of Bishops Wood, follow signs from A5 and A41, GR SJ837084. Use the English Heritage car park if visiting Boscobel House, otherwise park on the verge beside the lane
BUS/TRAIN:	None
REFRESHMENTS:	Tea Room at Boscobel House
MAP:	O.S. Explorer 242 – Telford, Ironbridge & The Wrekin

Starting at a house associated with Charles II's escape from Cromwell's troops in 1651, this easy paced walk takes you across pleasant and gently undulating countryside on the Shropshire-Staffordshire border. About half-way round you pass the impressive façade of Chillington Hall.

❶ Following his defeat at the battle of Worcester in September 1651, Charles II was on the run from Cromwell's soldiers and forced to go into hiding. After a few days

he arrived at Boscobel House, owned by a Royalist
sympathiser. The presence of so many of Cromwell's troops
in the vicinity made it dangerous to stay in the house
and he was forced to spend most of one day perched in
a nearby oak tree. He later headed southwards and after
many perilous adventures and a number of close shaves,
arrived on the south coast and escaped across the Channel.
He remained in exile for the next nine years until the
monarchy was restored in 1660.

Boscobel is a modest but interesting and picturesque
example of an early seventeenth-century timber-framed
house. Like many Catholic houses it has the usual priest

Boscobel House
Opposite: Track near Chillington Hall

holes and secret hiding places. The gardens are most
attractive and a short walk brings you to the Royal Oak.
This battered hulk is probably the descendant of the tree
in which Charles II hid as the original was destroyed by a
combination of bad weather and zealous souvenir hunters.
Tel: 01902 850 244

(ᛏ) ❶ **From the car park turn right to a T-junction and
turn right again. Keep along the road for about 2 km
(1.25 miles) – take care as there is not much of a verge
in places – and just over a slight brow, turn left, at a
public bridleway sign, along an enclosed track. Where the
track ends, keep ahead along a path by a wall bordering
Big Wood on the right.**

**The path later widens into a track again and gently
ascends to emerge, via a gate, onto a lane. Turn right
along the lane as far as a track on the left leading to
Chillington Farm. ❷ The route continues along this track
but it is worthwhile to keep ahead for another 800 m
(0.5 miles), following the lane around a right bend for a
visit to Chillington Hall and a good view of the façade of
the house.**

❶ The Chillington estate was once part of the medieval forest
of Brewood and has been owned by the Giffard family
since the twelfth century. The present house, a handsome
redbrick Georgian building, is the third on the site. It
was built in two stages, started in 1724 and completed
in the 1780s. The renowned architect Sir John Soane was
employed for the later work. The surrounding parkland was
landscaped by Capability Brown in the 1760s. Tel: 01902
850 236

(ᛏ) **Retrace your steps to point 2 and turn along the track
to Chillington Farm. Go through a gate, keep ahead,
follow the track around a left bend, passing in front of**

the farmhouse, and continue as far as a stile and public footpath sign on the right. Climb the stile, walk along the left edge of a field, by trees on the left, go through a gate and keep ahead across the next field to another stile. After climbing that, head gently uphill across a field and go through a gate onto a track in front of a farmhouse.

Turn left and walk along the enclosed, tree-lined track to a lane. ❸ Turn right, turn left at a T-junction and ignoring a right turn, follow the lane to the next T-junction. Turn right and take the first turn on the left to return to the start.

Boscobel House

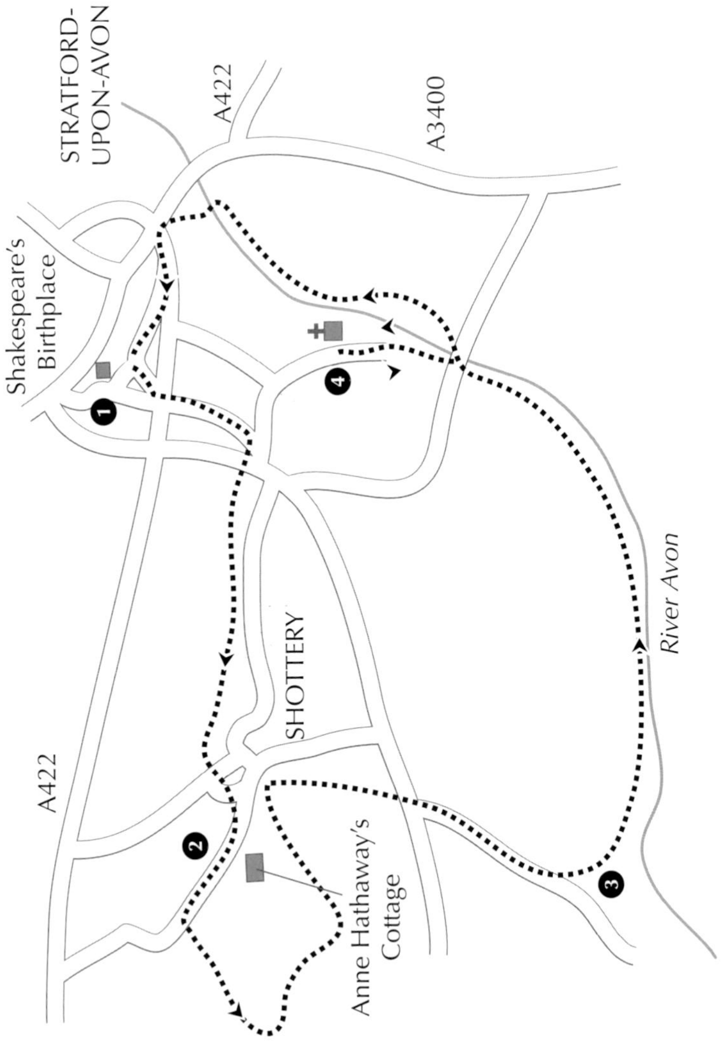

STRATFORD-
UPON-AVON

A422

A3400

Shakespeare's
Birthplace

1

4

River Avon

SHOTTERY

A422

2

3

Anne Hathaway's
Cottage

WALK 21

Shakespeare Country

LENGTH:	8.9 km (5.5 miles)
TIME:	2.5 hours
TERRAIN:	Flat walking on field and riverside paths
START/PARKING:	Stratford-upon-Avon, in front of Shakespeare's Birthplace in Henley Street, GR SP200552. Pay car parks in Stratford
BUS/TRAIN:	Buses from Birmingham, Leamington, Warwick, Oxford and most local towns and villages; trains from Birmingham
REFRESHMENTS:	Pubs and cafes at Stratford, cafes at Shottery
MAP:	O.S. Explorer 205 – Stratford-upon-Avon & Evesham

The main theme of this walk is not surprisingly William Shakespeare and the first part of it follows the route across fields from Stratford to Shottery – still pleasant despite being engulfed by Stratford's suburban expansion – which he probably took when visiting Anne Hathaway. From Shottery it continues to the banks of the River Avon and the last 3.2 km (2 miles) is a superb walk across meadows and parkland beside the river, with views of Holy Trinity church and the Royal Shakespeare Theatre on the opposite bank.

Shakespeare's birthplace

ℹ The fame and reputation of William Shakespeare draws thousands of visitors every year to Stratford-upon-Avon and most of them visit the house in Henley Street where he was born in 1564. His father John was a wool merchant and glove maker, active in local affairs, and the house is a typical sixteenth-century town house belonging to a reasonably well off businessman. Inside the main rooms are appropriately furnished and upstairs visitors can see the bedroom in which the playwright is supposed to have been born. Next to the Birthplace is the Shakespeare Centre, completed in 1964. Tel: 01789 204 016

There are many other places in Stratford associated with Shakespeare. The fifteenth-century Grammar School and adjoining Guild Chapel was where he went to school.

Hall's Croft was the early seventeenth-century home of
his daughter Susanna and her husband John Hall, an
eminent physician. New Place was the house where he
spent the latter part of his life and where he died in
1616. Unfortunately it was later demolished and only the
foundations and gardens remain but they form an attractive
oasis of calm in the bustling town. Towards the end of
the walk you pass by Holy Trinity church on the banks
of the Avon, where Shakespeare is buried, and the Royal
Shakespeare Theatre, built in 1932 to replace a Victorian
predecessor destroyed by fire.

Although at first glance you may not think so, there is
more to Stratford than Shakespeare. It is a most appealing
town in its own right and with its superb riverside location
and extensive collection of black and white Tudor buildings
– more than almost any other town in the country – it
would still be a major tourist attraction.

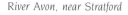

River Avon, near Stratford

🚶 ❶ Facing Shakespeare's Birthplace, turn right along Henley Street and take the first turn on the right (Meer Street). Cross over at a road junction and continue down Rother Street into Evesham Place. At a road junction by a triangular traffic island, turn right – there is a footpath sign to Anne Hathaway's Cottage – cross Grove Road and take the enclosed tarmac track ahead.

Shakespeare is buried in Holy Trinity church on the banks of the Avon at Stratford

After keeping ahead at a crossways, the route continues in a straight line along enclosed paths, crossing a succession of suburban roads, before heading across the middle of a playing field. At a fork, take the right hand path to the far right corner of the field, walk along a narrow enclosed path and at the next fork, continue along the right hand path, signposted "Anne Hathaway's Cottage via Tavern Lane", to emerge onto a lane.

Keep ahead into Shottery, passing Dudfield's Nurseries and Coffee Shop, and at a crossroads, bear right to go up steps and take a path that runs parallel to Cottage Lane. The path bends right alongside Shottery Brook and turns left over a footbridge to emerge onto the lane opposite Anne Hathaway's Cottage. ❷

ℹ️ As the childhood home of Shakespeare's wife, Anne Hathaway's Cottage is obviously a major attraction for Shakespeare enthusiasts. Although called a cottage, this half-timbered, thatched building is more of a farmhouse as the Hathaways were a family of reasonably prosperous yeomen farmers. Parts of it date from the fifteenth century and the various rooms contain authentic Tudor furniture and utensils. Anne Hathaway was 8 years older than William and they were married in 1582 when he was 18 and she was 26. Tel: 01789 292 100

🚶 Turn right and at a public footpath sign to Hansell Farm, turn left along an enclosed tarmac drive. Where the drive bends left, turn sharp left over a stile and walk along the right edge of a field. Go through a gate in the corner and continue along a path which turns left, heading gently downhill, and then curves right to the field edge. From this path there are fine views over Stratford and the Avon valley.

Keep ahead through bushes and trees to a T-junction and turn left along a tree-lined path which leads back to

Royal Shakespeare Theatre

the edge of Shottery. Just after emerging onto a track, turn right along a hedge-lined path to a road. Continue along it (Hogarth Road) and where it ends, keep ahead along an enclosed tree-lined path beside Shottery Brook to a road. Carefully cross the main road and take the road opposite (Luddington Road), passing to the right of Stratford Racecourse. At a right curve, turn left along Stannells Close and where the road ends, turn left along an enclosed path which bends first right and then left to the River Avon. ❸

The remainder of the route is along delightful riverside paths. Initially you walk along the left bank of the Avon, passing under a disused railway bridge and later under a road bridge. After going under the road bridge, keep ahead to emerge onto a road and Holy Trinity Church, where Shakespeare is buried, is just ahead. ❹

ⓘ Holy Trinity church was built in the early thirteenth century and lies in a beautiful setting by the Avon. Shakespeare was both baptised here in 1564 and buried here in 1616. His grave and those of other members of his family can be seen at the east end of the church.

🚶 **Return to the road bridge but just before reaching it, turn left to cross a footbridge over the Avon and turn left to continue along the other bank. The route follows a well-surfaced path across Bancroft Gardens, with superb views across the river of Holy Trinity Church and later the Royal Shakespeare Theatre, eventually reaching a T-junction to the right of the Tramway Bridge.**

Turn left to cross the bridge, keep ahead to a road and bear left, passing Shakespeare's statue and crossing a bridge over the canal. Continue up the broad Bridge Street and at a road junction, bear slightly right along Henley Street to return to Shakespeare's Birthplace.

River Avon at Stratford

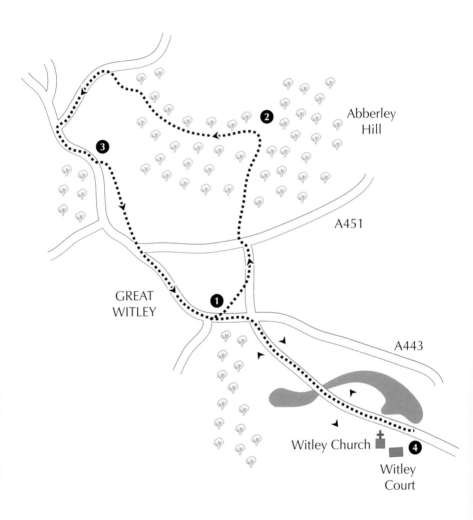

WALK 22

Abberley Hill and Witley Court

LENGTH:	8.9 km (5.5 miles)
TIME:	2.5 hours
TERRAIN:	A steep ascent and descent through woodland followed by an easy flat walk along a lane
START/PARKING:	Great Witley, Village Hall car park at the junction of the A443 and B4197, GR SO757657
BUS/TRAIN:	Occasional buses from Worcester and Tenbury Wells
REFRESHMENTS:	Pub at Great Witley, tea room at Witley church
MAP:	O.S. Explorer 204 – Worcester & Droitwich Spa

The thickly wooded slopes of the Abberley Hills rise to over 274 m (900 feet) above the Teme valley and provide a series of superb views from their higher points. The first part of the route is a stiff climb up to the ridge of Abberley Hill followed by a walk along the ridge to the summit and a descent to the start. Then comes a 'there and back' walk along a lane to the magnificent and stately ruins of Witley Court and the unusually ornate adjacent church.

(🚶) ❶ Turn left out of the car park, immediately turn left again through a kissing gate, at a public footpath sign, and head diagonally across a field. In the far corner, go through a gap onto a road and turn left to a T-junction. Turn left and at a public bridleway sign to Shavers End, turn right along a track.

At a blue-waymarked post, keep ahead uphill along a tree-lined path, cross a track and head more steeply uphill through the thick woodland that clothes the slopes of Abberley Hill. At a fork, take the right hand path and continue up to the ridge to reach a waymarked post at a crossways. ❷ Turn left and follow the ridge path, still climbing – to the trig point on the summit.

(ℹ) At a height of 283 m (928 feet), the summit of Abberley Hill is the highest point on the range. From here the magnificent views take in Woodbury Hill, another hill in the range and site of an Iron Age fort, and extend across the Teme valley to the outline of the Malverns. The most outstanding landmark is a tall Victorian clock tower known locally as 'Jones' Folly', erected in 1883 by John Joseph Jones of Abberley Hall as a memorial to his father.

(🚶) As you continue along the ridge, fine views can also be seen through the trees on the right. The path descends quite steeply to emerge onto a lane. Turn left downhill to the A443, turn left and where the road bends right, turn left up a tarmac track, at a public footpath sign to Witley Hill. ❸ At the next public footpath sign turn right along a track and look out for the next one where you turn right again onto a wooded path which descends to a stile.

Climb it and bear slightly left across a field, making for a stile on the left hand side. After climbing that – and another immediately ahead – continue diagonally downhill across the next field and go through a hedge gap in the far left corner. Walk down a track beside the

View over Worcestershire from the slopes of the Abberley Hills

Hundred House Hotel to the A443 again and turn left.
Where the road forks, continue along the right hand road
(still the A443 and signposted to Worcester) and follow it
back to the start. ❶

For the extension to Witley Court, continue past the
car park and turn right along the lane signposted to
Witley Church. After nearly 1.6 km (1 mile) you reach the
adjacent church and ruined house. ❹

ⓘ An English Heritage leaflet describes Witley Court as 'Once
one of England's great country houses, today an evocative
and spectacular ruin'. Although a ruin, the extent and
setting of the remains still manage to convey something of
the elegance and grandeur of this large Italianate palace in

Witley's eighteenth-century Baroque church

its Victorian and Edwardian heyday when it was owned by the earls of Dudley.

The house was built in 1655 by Thomas Foley on the site of an earlier modest manor house. A major reconstruction was carried out by John Nash in the early nineteenth century but in 1837 debts forced the Foleys to sell the estate. It was bought by the Wards, later the earls of Dudley, a family made wealthy by the exploitation of the coal and iron resources of the Black Country. By the middle of the nineteenth century the noise and smoke of the Black Country had started to encroach on their existing estate at Himley Hall and they decided to seek rural peace and solitude here. The 1st Earl of Dudley had the house transformed into a vast Italian-style palace and also had the grounds landscaped.

Following the decline of the Dudley family fortunes, the estate was sold again in 1920, this time to a Kidderminster carpet manufacturer. Disaster struck in 1937 when the house was gutted by fire and reduced to ruins. After a succession of owners and years of uncertainty, during which it was nearly demolished, Witley Court was acquired by English Heritage in 1972. Since then the ruins have been cleared and stabilised and the grounds, with their ornamental gardens, fountains, lake and woodlands have been restored to something approaching their former glory. Tel: 01299 896 636

The adjacent church, built by the 1st Lord Foley in 1735, fortunately survived the fire. It is a rare example of an English Baroque church – a style more usually found in northern Italy, southern Germany and Austria – and has an unusually rich and ornate interior with gold and white colouring, painted ceiling and eighteenth-century stained-glass windows.

From here retrace your steps along the lane to return to the car park at Great Witley.

The splendid ruins of Witley Court

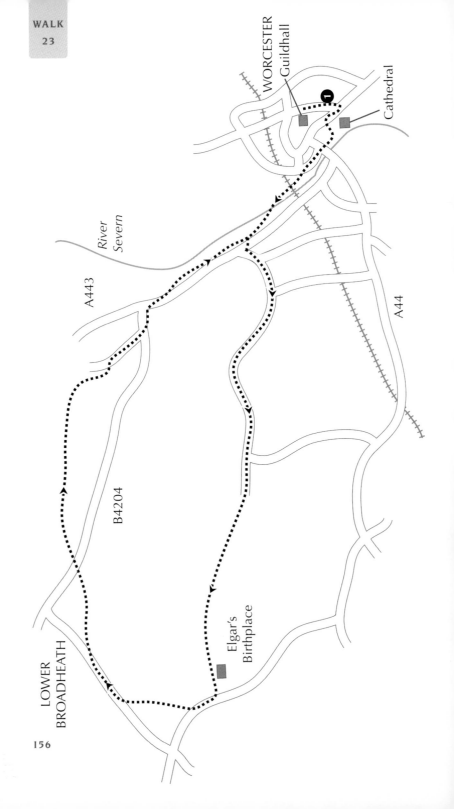

WALK 23

Worcester and Elgar Country

LENGTH:	12.9 km (8 miles)
TIME:	4 hours
TERRAIN:	Flat and easy walking along roads and riverside and field paths
START/PARKING:	Worcester, the Guildhall, GR SO850549. Plenty of pay car parks at Worcester
BUS/TRAIN:	Buses and trains from Birmingham, Kidderminster, Great Malvern and Evesham
REFRESHMENTS:	Pubs and cafes at Worcester, pub by the Elgar Birthplace Museum
MAP:	O.S. Explorer 204 – Worcester & Droitwich Spa

The walk has a strong Elgar theme. It starts close to a statue to England's greatest composer by Worcester Cathedral and takes you by field paths and tracks, roads and riverside paths to his birthplace at Lower Broadheath. Views over the Severn valley and across fields to Elgar's beloved Malvern Hills, plus attractive riverside walking, more than compensate for some walking along suburban roads when leaving and returning to the cathedral city.

① Facing the ornate façade of the early eighteenth-century Guildhall, one of Worcester's finest buildings, turn left along the pedestrianised High Street to the statue of Sir Edward Elgar in front of the cathedral.

ℹ The most memorable views of Worcester Cathedral are from the west, the well-proportioned west front and imposing central tower rising above the Severn seen from

Worcester's early eighteenth-century Guildhall

Tower of Worcester Cathedral and the statue of Elgar

either Worcester Bridge or from the other side of the river. The cathedral was begun in the late eleventh century by St Wulstan, the only Anglo-Saxon bishop to retain his job after the Norman Conquest. A series of disasters in the twelfth century – two fires and the collapse of the tower – means that little is left of the Norman church except for the superb crypt and chapter house.

The cathedral was rebuilt in the Gothic style in the thirteenth and fourteenth centuries and, despite

Worcester Bridge and opposite, Worcester Cathedral

considerable Victorian restoration, the completion of the central tower in 1374 left the building much as it is today. Two monuments claim particular attention. One is the tomb of King John who was buried here in 1216, his fatal illness probably brought on by the loss of the Crown Jewels while crossing The Wash. The other is the elaborate Prince Arthur's Chantry, commemorating the eldest son of Henry VII and first husband of Catherine of Aragon who was buried here. But for his early death in 1502, his younger brother, the future Henry VIII, might never have come to the throne. Tel: 01905 28854

At Elgar's statue turn right along Deansway and turn left between the buildings of the College of Technology and the tower and spire of St Andrews church – all that is left of the building – down to the River Severn. Turn right

to Worcester Bridge, constructed in the early eighteenth century, cross a road, keep ahead and descend steps to leave the road and continue through delightful riverside gardens. About 91 m (100 yards) after passing under a railway bridge, turn left to cross a footbridge over the river and turn right to continue along the other bank.

Turn left in front of a gate to the A443, cross over and head uphill along the enclosed tarmac path ahead (Holywell Hill) to a road. ❷ Cross that and continue

Field path near Lower Broadheath

Birthplace of Sir Edward Elgar in 1857

along the road ahead (Oldbury Road) for about 2 km
(1.25 miles) of suburban road walking. Beyond the last of
the houses, the road narrows to a lane and where that
ends at a fork, take the left hand enclosed path. Over to
the left the outline of the Malverns can be seen. After
passing beside a gate, keep ahead along a tarmac track
to a T-junction, go through a gate and continue along a
tree-lined tarmac track. Where the track bends left, keep
ahead through a gate and walk along an enclosed path to
a road. Turn right and right again beside the Plough Inn
to reach the entrance to the Elgar Birthplace Museum. ❸

ⓘ The Elgar Birthplace Museum comprises two buildings: the modest house in which the composer was born in 1857 and a new Elgar Centre – opened in 2000 – which was needed to house and display the increasing number of exhibits and to provide better facilities for visitors than the somewhat cramped birthplace. Both buildings are full of memorabilia and contain a wealth of information on the life and work of one of England's greatest composers.

The house, which became a museum after Elgar's death in 1934, is particularly atmospheric. It overlooks the gentle Worcestershire countryside with views towards his beloved Malvern Hills, the inspiration for much of his music.

Tel: 01905 333 224

Ⓚ Continue past the pub and at a public bridleway sign, turn right along Laylocks Lane beside Broadheath Common. At the next public bridleway sign where the lane bears right, keep ahead across the common, making for the far right corner where you emerge onto a road at a T-junction. Turn right and on reaching the first of the houses on the right, turn right onto a track and almost immediately turn left and walk along a left field edge. At a hedge corner turn right, walk across the field towards woodland and follow the path through the trees, later continuing along a track to a road.

Turn right and at a public bridleway sign, turn left along a track to a gate. Go through, keep ahead along the right edge of a field, go through another gate, cross a lane and go through the gate opposite. The way continues initially along a right field edge, then heads between fields and later keeps along a left field edge. After joining a tarmac track, continue along it and where it bends left to a house, keep ahead, at a public bridleway sign, along a hedge-lined track to a gate.

Go through, bear right and head gently downhill across a field, keeping parallel to its right edge. Climb

a stile in the corner, keep ahead through trees, cross
a footbridge over a stream and ascend a flight of steps
to emerge onto a road. ❹ Turn right and the road
(Monarch Drive) curves gradually left and then curves
right to a T-junction. Turn left along Martley Road to
another T-junction and turn right along the A443. Just
after passing King Stephen's Mount on the left, bear
left downhill along a tarmac path which curves left and
continues down to the river. ❺

Turn right beside the Severn and follow it back into
Worcester, soon getting a view of the cathedral tower.
After passing through the fourth in a sequence of gates,
you rejoin the outward route and retrace your steps to
the start.

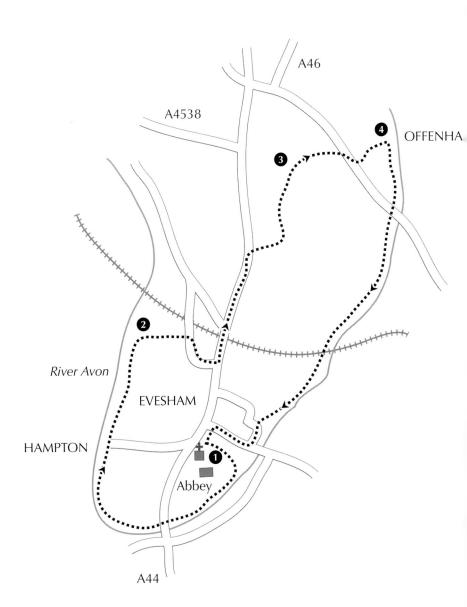

A46

A4538

OFFENHA

❹

❸

River Avon

❷

EVESHAM

HAMPTON

❶

Abbey

A44

WALK 24

Battle of Evesham

LENGTH:	9.7 km (6 miles)
TIME:	3 hours
TERRAIN:	Apart from a section along a road and a few field paths, most of the route is across riverside meadows
START/PARKING:	Evesham, Market Place, GR SP037436. Pay car parks at Evesham
BUS/TRAIN:	Buses from Birmingham, Worcester, Stratford-upon-Avon, Redditch and Cheltenham; trains from Worcester and Oxford
REFRESHMENTS:	Pubs and cafes at Evesham
MAP:	O.S. Explorer 205 – Stratford-upon-Avon & Evesham

The River Avon does a horseshoe loop around Evesham and the first part of the walk follows this loop around the southern and western sides of the town before heading back across the narrowest part of the horseshoe to the town centre. After a stretch along a road, paths and tracks take you at first above the Avon valley and then down to the banks of the river. The final leg follows the eastern side of the loop back to the start. Apart from the churches and monastic remains at Evesham, the theme of this walk is the battle that was fought around the town in 1265 and the route passes some of the main physical reminders of that conflict.

(walker) **❶ Facing the main road, turn left and go through the Abbey Gateway into the precincts of the former abbey. Follow the path to the left between the two churches, pass under the Bell Tower and descend to the River Avon.**

(i) Of the once powerful Evesham Abbey, founded in 714, virtually nothing is left apart from the imposing detached Bell Tower. This was built in the early sixteenth century by the last abbot and had hardly been completed before the abbey was dissolved. The only other monastic survivals are the Abbey Gateway and fourteenth-century Almonry, the latter now a museum and tourist information centre with displays on the Battle of Evesham. A memorial stone placed in what was the east end of the abbey marks the alleged grave of Simon de Montfort, leader of the revolt against Henry III who was killed in the battle.

Unusually there are two churches within the precincts of the former abbey, St Lawrence's and All Saints. Both are impressive buildings with spires rising above their west towers.

(walker) **Turn right along the tarmac, tree-lined riverside path and after going under a road bridge, the river curves gradually right to the Hampton Ferry. Continue past the ferry to join a lane and where that ends, keep ahead along a track, passing sports fields on the right. Where the track ends, turn right ❷ along the left edge of a sports field, by a brook on the left, and in the corner turn left over a stile.**

Turn right gently uphill along an enclosed path, turn right again along a tarmac drive and bear right on joining a road. Take the first road on the left to a T-junction at the top of Evesham High Street and turn left. Cross a railway bridge near the station and continue up Greenhill.

Opposite: The Bell Tower is all that is left of Evesham Abbey

The stone marks the alleged grave of Simon de Montfort at the east end of the vanished abbey church

ℹ️ The area around Greenhill was the heart of the battle of Evesham and the scene of much slaughter. The battle, fought on 4 August 1265, was the climax of a long period of tension between Henry III and some of his leading barons.

In 1264 rising discontent against the king spearheaded by Simon de Montfort resulted in the so-called Barons War. During this war Henry and his son Prince Edward – the future Edward I – were defeated at the battle of Lewes and the king became more or less a puppet ruler under the control of Simon de Montfort and his allies.

Prince Edward was held as a hostage to Henry's co-operation but in May 1265 he managed to escape and forged an alliance with some of De Montfort's chief opponents, notably the powerful Gilbert de Clare, Earl of Gloucester. Simon de Montfort was in Hereford and decided to move to his stronghold at Kenilworth Castle. Prince Edward, who was at Worcester, set off to intercept him. On 3 August De Montfort arrived at Evesham and set up camp there unaware that Edward was so close. He

could not have picked a worse place. The horseshoe loop
that the River Avon does around Evesham affords some
protection but at the same time makes it easy for an enemy
to surround and block possible escape routes. On the
following morning Simon de Montfort realised that he was
caught in a trap when a look out on the top of the abbey
tower warned him that large numbers of the enemy were
converging on the town.

Taking advantage of his far greater numbers, Edward split
his forces into three to cut off all the likely escape routes.
He and Gloucester positioned themselves either side of
the low ridge of Greenhill to the north of the town, the
only way out without having to cross the river, and Roger
Mortimer was sent to guard Bengeworth Bridge, the only
bridge over the Avon. De Montfort decided that his only
hope was to storm his way through the main bulk of the

River Avon at Evesham

The Avon at Offenham; many of Simon de Montfort's troops were slaughtered in these meadows while attempting to flee from the battle

enemy army and force his way over Greenhill but the two wings of Edward's army that were camped there swept down on his troops and the result was a massacre. Some of De Montfort's Welsh allies tried to flee by swimming across the Avon near Offenham Bridge but most of these were either drowned or killed by enemy forces.

Simon de Montfort himself was killed in the fierce fighting. Henry III was fully reinstated as king and seven years later was succeeded by his son, Edward I.

Head over the brow and look out for a public footpath sign where you turn right along an enclosed path. Soon fine views open up across the Vale of Evesham to the western escarpment of the Cotswolds. Follow the path around a left bend to continue above the valley, by a hedge on the left, and in the field corner turn right to

a gate. Go through, keep ahead along an enclosed path to a T-junction ❸ and turn right gently downhill along a tarmac, tree-lined track.

Where the track bends right, keep ahead along an enclosed path. In front of a fence, bear right over a stile, keep along the left edge of a field to a tarmac drive and turn left to cross carefully the busy A46. Take the track opposite and look out for where you turn right through a kissing gate. Head down an embankment and walk straight across a meadow to reach the River Avon opposite the Bridge Inn at Offenham. ❹

🛈 At the time of the battle there was a bridge here which no longer exists. In the meadows near this spot, subsequently known as Dead Man's Ait, there was much slaughter as many of Simon de Montfort's Welsh allies tried to escape from the carnage of the battle by swimming across the river. They were either drowned or killed by the enemy.

🚶 Turn right beside the river and follow it across meadows back into Evesham, going through a succession of gates and passing under the A46 and a railway bridge. Approaching the town, you emerge onto a track but where it curves right, bear left to continue beside the Avon. Eventually the path bears right to reach a road. Turn left and bear left on joining another road to a T-junction.

🛈 To the left is Bengeworth Bridge, a modern successor of the bridge that was held by Roger Mortimer at the time of the battle to block one of Simon de Montfort's possible escape routes. At the time it was the only bridge across the river out of Evesham.

🚶 Turn right up the pedestrianised Bridge Street and at the top turn left to return to the Market Place.

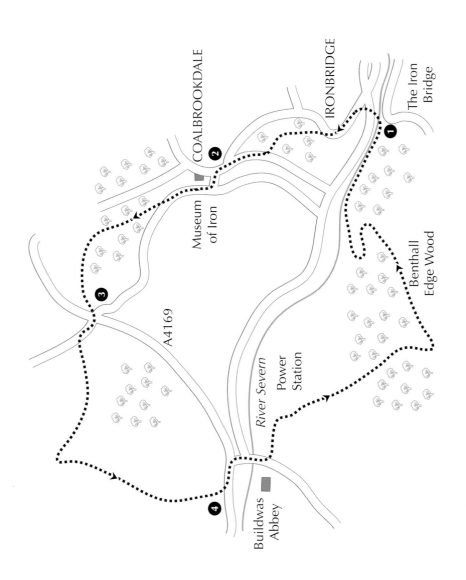

WALK 25

Ironbridge Gorge, Coalbrookdale and Buildwas Abbey

LENGTH:	12.9 km (8 miles)
TIME:	4 hours
TERRAIN:	Quite a hilly walk with several climbs and descents and a particularly steep descent down a long flight of steps near the end; varied mixture of woodland and open country
START/PARKING:	Ironbridge, south side of the Iron Bridge, GR SJ672033. Pay car park on the south side of the Iron Bridge
BUS/TRAIN:	Buses from Telford town centre and Shrewsbury
REFRESHMENTS:	Pubs and cafes at Ironbridge, pubs at Coalbrookdale, café at the Museum of Iron at Coalbrookdale
MAP:	O.S. Explorer 242 – Telford, Ironbridge & The Wrekin

There are a series of superb views, a variety of terrain and a wealth of historic interest throughout the route. It starts and finishes in the Ironbridge Gorge, a uniquely fascinating area and one of the major birthplaces of the Industrial Revolution, and passes such industrial icons as the Iron Bridge and the site of Abraham Darby's foundry

at Coalbrookdale. As a complete contrast, the walk also
includes the ruins of a medieval abbey. Scenically there are
fine views of The Wrekin and the Severn valley and some
splendid woodland walking, especially on the final descent
along the side of the gorge.

In 1709 Abraham Darby, a Quaker ironmaster from
Coalbrookdale, first successfully developed the technique of
smelting iron ore using coke instead of charcoal to generate
the extreme heat needed in the process. It was this
event which both revolutionised the industry and focused
attention on this little known part of Shropshire. Up to then
iron had been dependent on supplies of timber – which
were fast running out – but now it could use coal, of
which there was plenty, and expand and extend its range.

By the middle of the eighteenth century Coalbrookdale
and the Severn gorge had become major centres of the
iron industry. This increased trade led local ironmasters, led
by Abraham Darby III and John Wilkinson, to demand the
building of a new bridge across the Severn and Pritchard
was commissioned to design one to be built of iron. The
iron bridge was completed in 1779, the first of its kind in

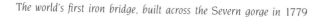

The world's first iron bridge, built across the Severn gorge in 1779

the world, and immediately aroused immense interest and enthusiasm. Visitors came from all over Europe to gaze at it and the other wonders of the gorge and a town grew up on its north side.

In the nineteenth century the iron industry moved away to the more abundant coal deposits of south Staffordshire (the Black Country) not far away and Ironbridge declined as an industrial area. Now it has been revitalised as a major tourist attraction and is one of Britain's World Heritage Sites. The bridge itself is the focal point of a whole series of industrial monuments and museums scattered throughout the gorge and the adjacent valley of Coalbrookdale and the whole area can justifiably claim to be one of the cradles of the Industrial Revolution.

For information about the various sites in the Ironbridge Gorge phone 01952 884 391

❶ Start by turning right out of the car park and cross the Iron Bridge. The Tollhouse at the south end of the bridge is now an information centre. Keeping to the right of the Tontine Inn opposite, climb a flight of steps, pass under an arch to emerge onto a road and turn left beside Ironbridge church. The road curves right and at a footpath post by a fork, turn sharp left along a track and turn right, at another public footpath sign, onto a path through woodland.

At a junction of paths, bear right, in the Paradise direction, to a fork immediately in front and take the left hand lower path. Bear left downhill at the next footpath sign, still in the direction of Paradise, continue down steps and then curve left to walk down an enclosed tarmac track to a road. Turn right and keep ahead on joining the main road through Coalbrookdale. Take the first road on the left ❷ which bends left, passing the Museum of Iron, and continues under a disused railway bridge to a T-junction.

The Iron Bridge now lies at the heart of a fascinating World Heritage Site

ℹ️ The Museum of Iron is a major shrine to industry as it stands on the site of the blast furnace where in 1709 Abraham Darby first smelted iron using coke instead of charcoal. Over the following century the ironworks rolled out wheels, rails and all kinds of machine parts and later on in the nineteenth century became renowned for its decorative cast iron objects. The Old Furnace, protected from the weather by a modern building, can be seen and in the Warehouse are displays and artefacts, as well as a shop and café. Nearby are the Darby Houses, former homes of the family of ironmasters.

🚶 **Turn right at the T-junction and at the next T-junction by Upper Furnace Pool, turn left uphill, passing the Darby Houses. At a public footpath sign to Ropewalk, bear right through a gate and walk along a track through the lovely woodland of Loamhole Dingle. Pass through a fence gap into the equally beautiful adjacent woodland of Lydebrook Dingle and cross a footbridge. Climb a series of steps along the edge of the valley and at the top, turn** left and continue up through woodland to a stile at the top edge of the trees. Climb it, keep ahead across a field, go through a gate to the left of a house and turn left along a tarmac track which curves left to a lane.

Turn right, ❸ cross a bridge over the A4169 and continue along the lane. At public footpath and Shropshire Way signs, turn left along an enclosed track, pass to the right of a farmhouse and look out for where you turn right over a stile just in front of a gate. Head diagonally across a field and bear right on the far side to keep along its left edge to a stile. Climb it, keep in the same direction across the next field and on the far side, climb a stile and turn left downhill along a sunken track. At the bottom, bear left along a tarmac track down to a road. ❹

Turn left and take the first road on the right to cross Buildwas Bridge over the River Severn. About 92 m (100 yards) further on, keep ahead to visit Buildwas Abbey but the route continues to the left along a tarmac track parallel to a railway line.

The Museum of Iron at Coalbrookdale stands on the site of the blast furnace where Abraham Darby first smelted iron with coke in 1709

🛈 The ruins of Buildwas Abbey lie in a secluded position on the banks of the River Severn. Founded in 1135 and dissolved by Henry VIII in 1536, it was one of the smaller English monasteries and had a relatively uneventful existence apart from being subjected to several raids from across the Welsh border. The remains are substantial, especially the nave of the twelfth-century church with its massive Norman arches. The vaulted chapter house is also impressive. Tel: 01952 433274

🚶 **The track bends right and heads uphill, beside the perimeter fence of Ironbridge Power Station on the left. Continue between a caravan park and chalet bungalows and where the tarmac track bends left, keep ahead to go through a gate. Head uphill along a track through woodland – it later narrows to a path – negotiate a series of gates and stiles in quick succession and continue steeply up to a T-junction.**

Turn left to rejoin the Shropshire Way. ❺ After climbing a stile, keep ahead to join another track and immediately turn sharp left along it, bending right to a gate. Go through, keep ahead by the right inside edge of Benthall Edge Wood and at a Shropshire Way post by a cottage, turn left into the woodland. Follow a winding and well-waymarked downhill path through the Severn Gorge – there are striking views of the pink sandstone cooling towers of the power station – and at a fork, take the left hand path to reach the top of a flight of steps.

Turn left to commence a long descent down these steps, turning sharp left and heading back towards the cooling towers. Later the steps bend right to continue down to the bottom of the gorge where you turn right onto a path above the river. The path descends, passes through a fence gap and bears left to a track. Turn right to return to the starting point.